WOLVES
Coloring Book For Kids

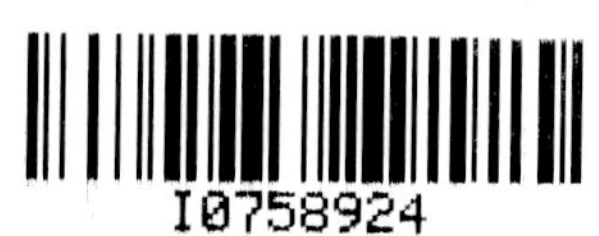

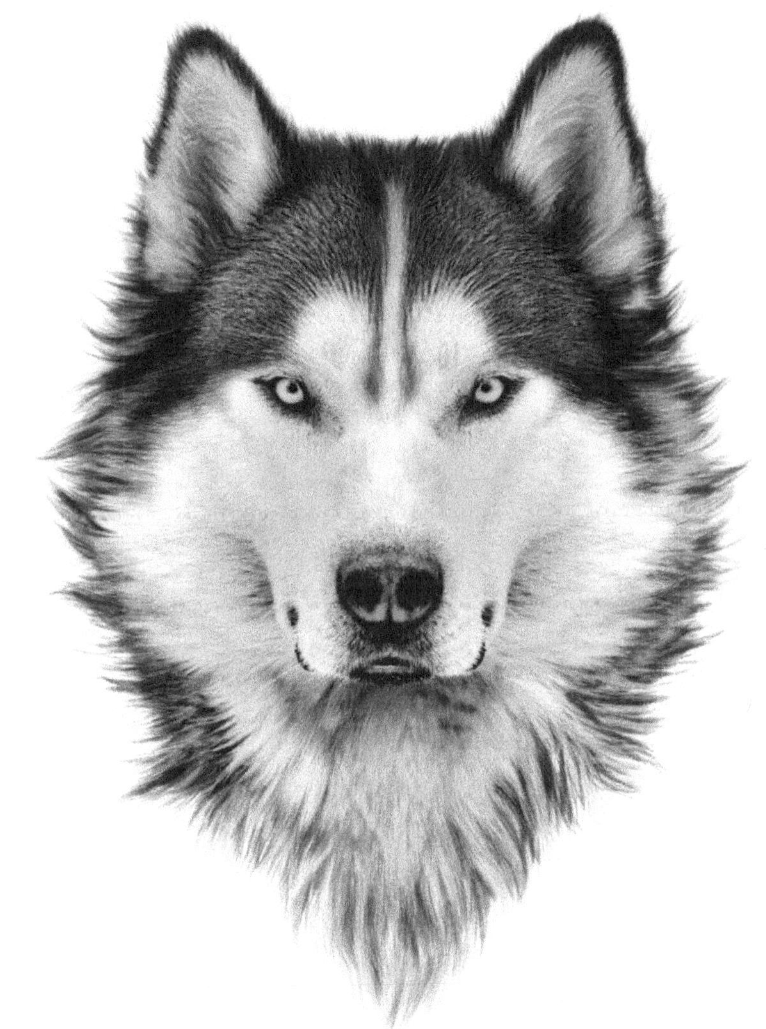

52 Amazing Wolves Coloring Pages

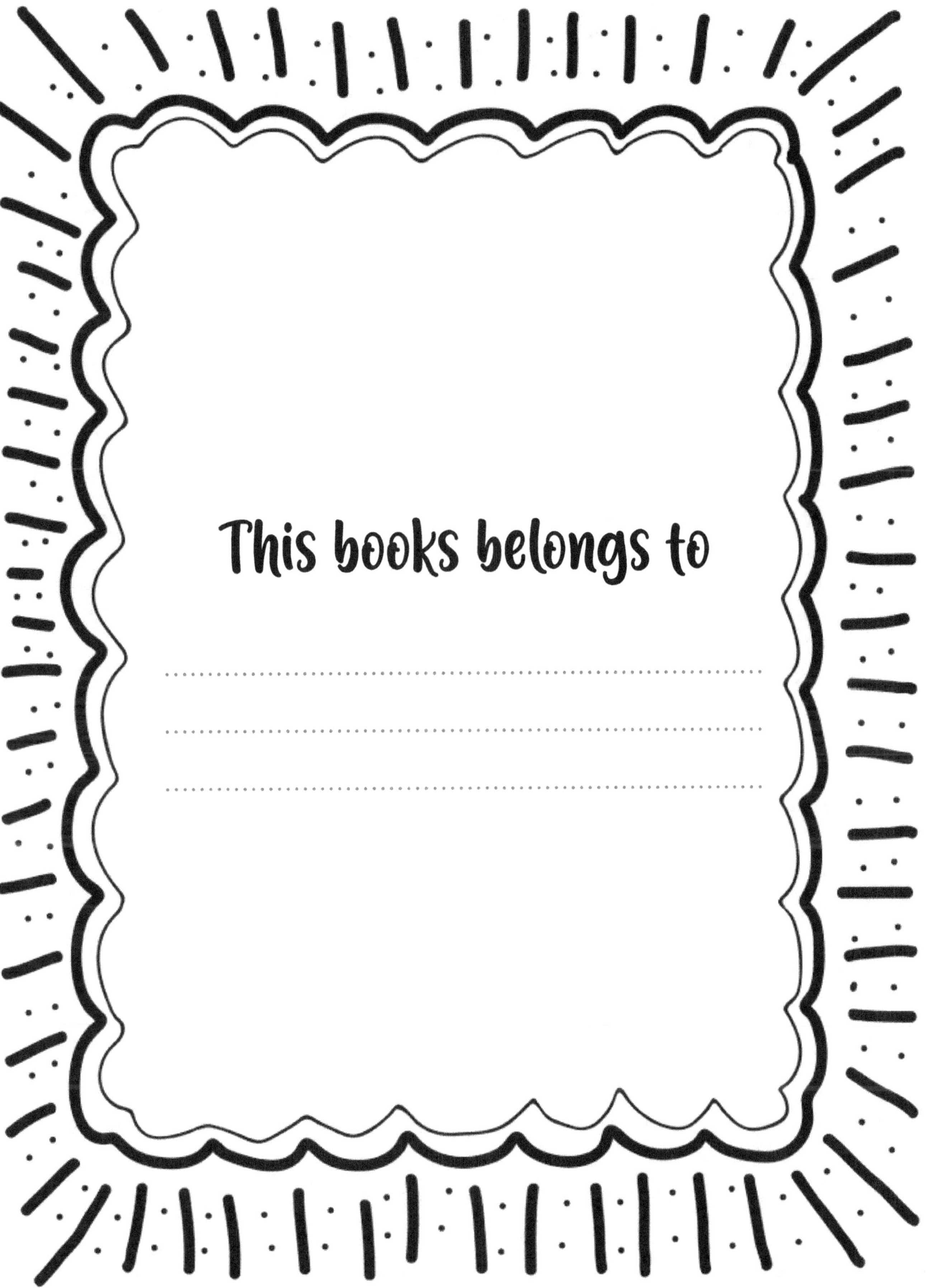
This books belongs to

Color Test Page

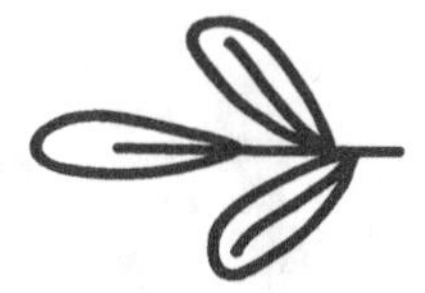
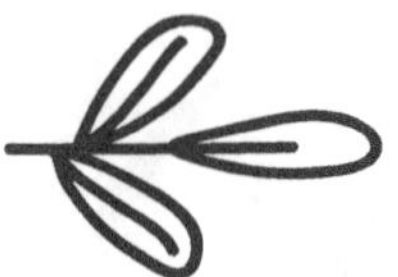

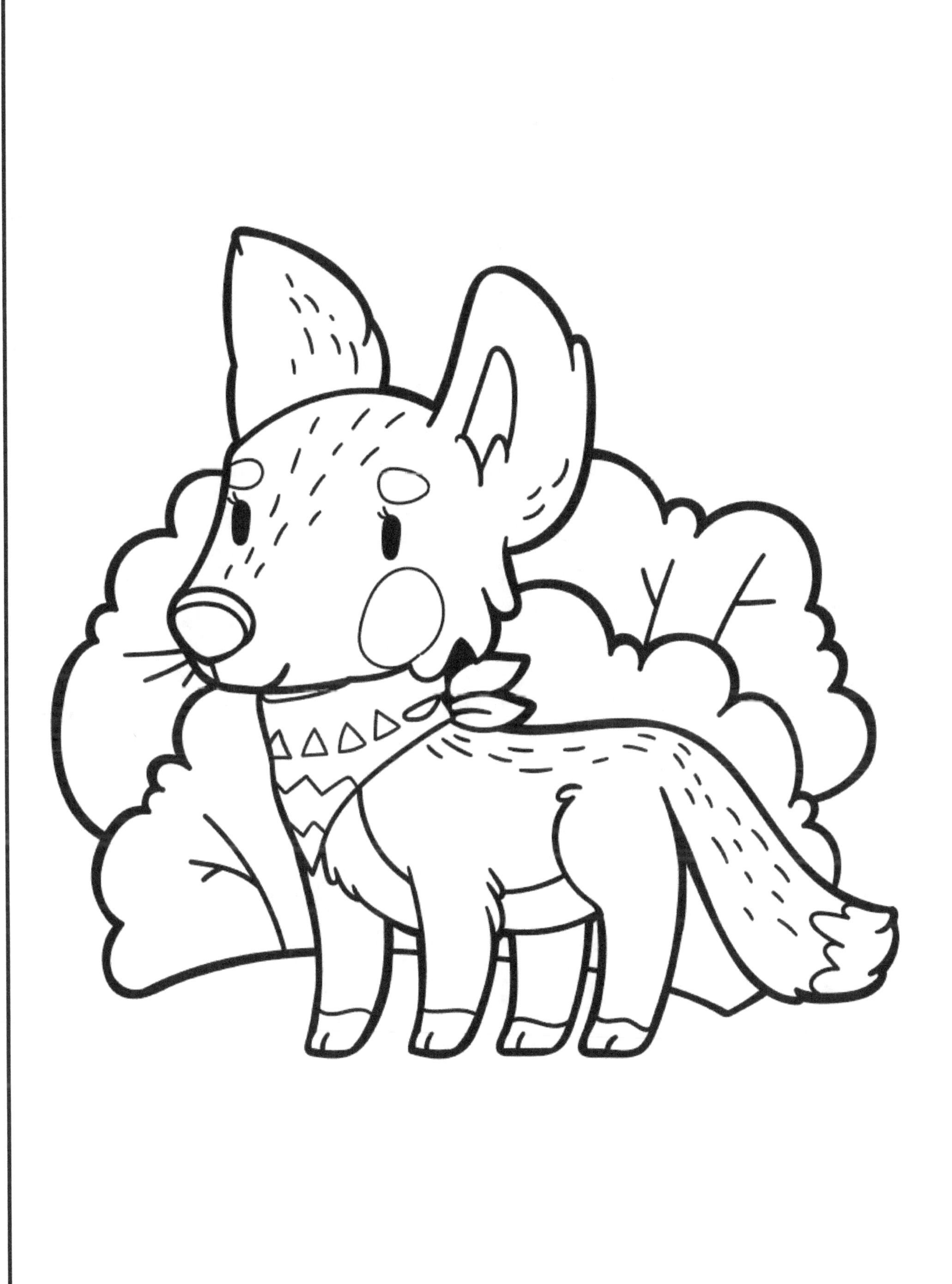

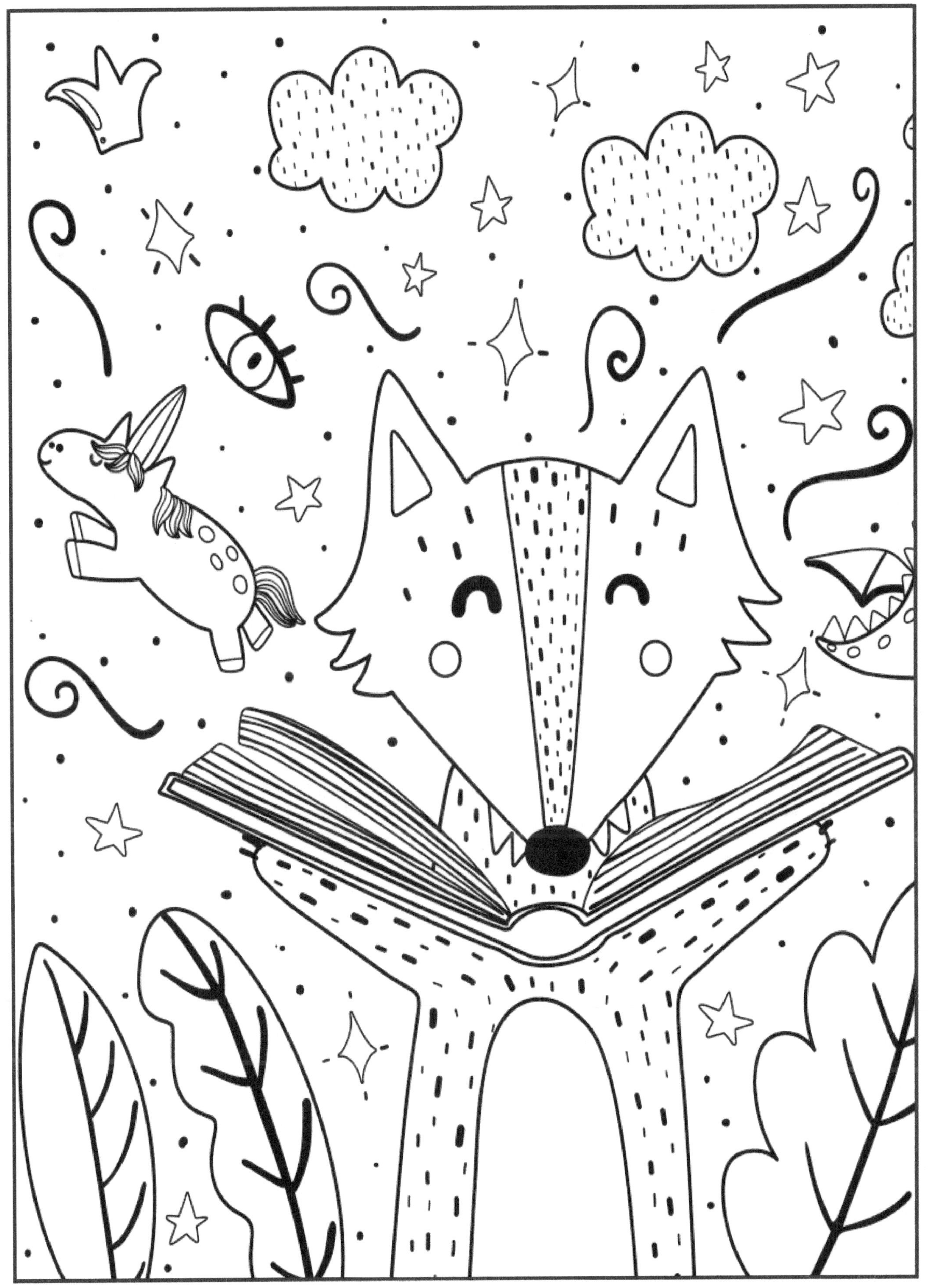

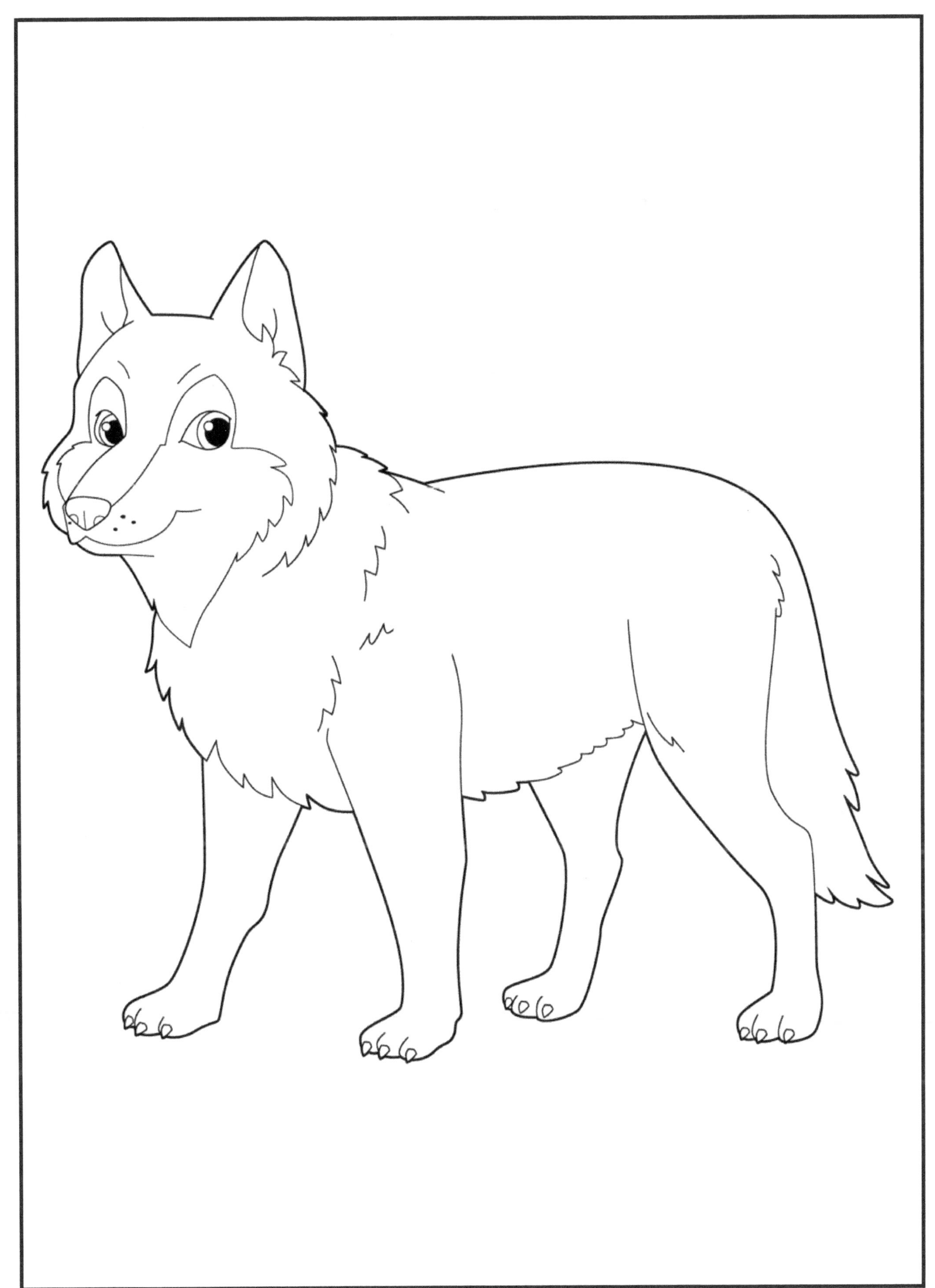

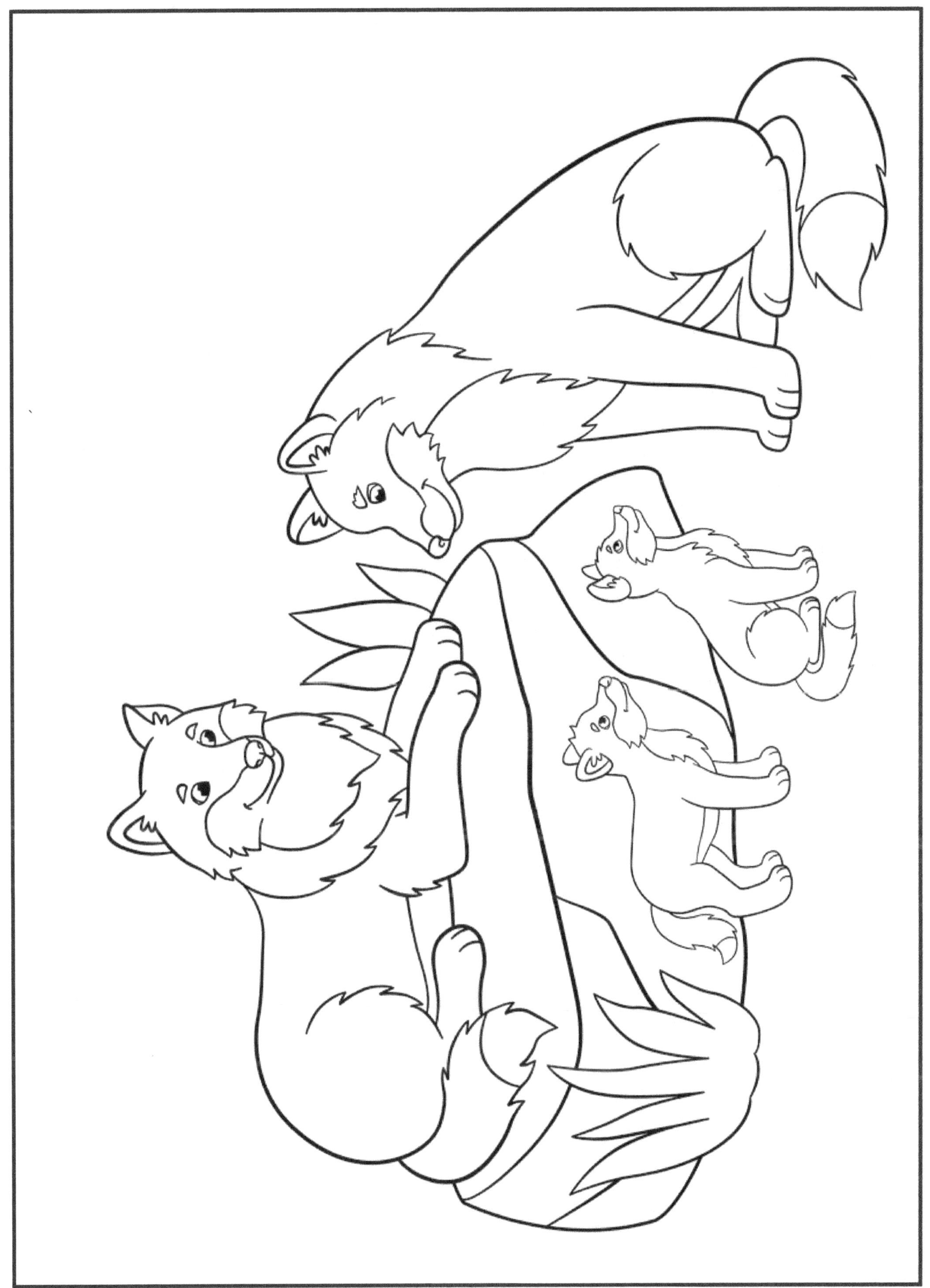

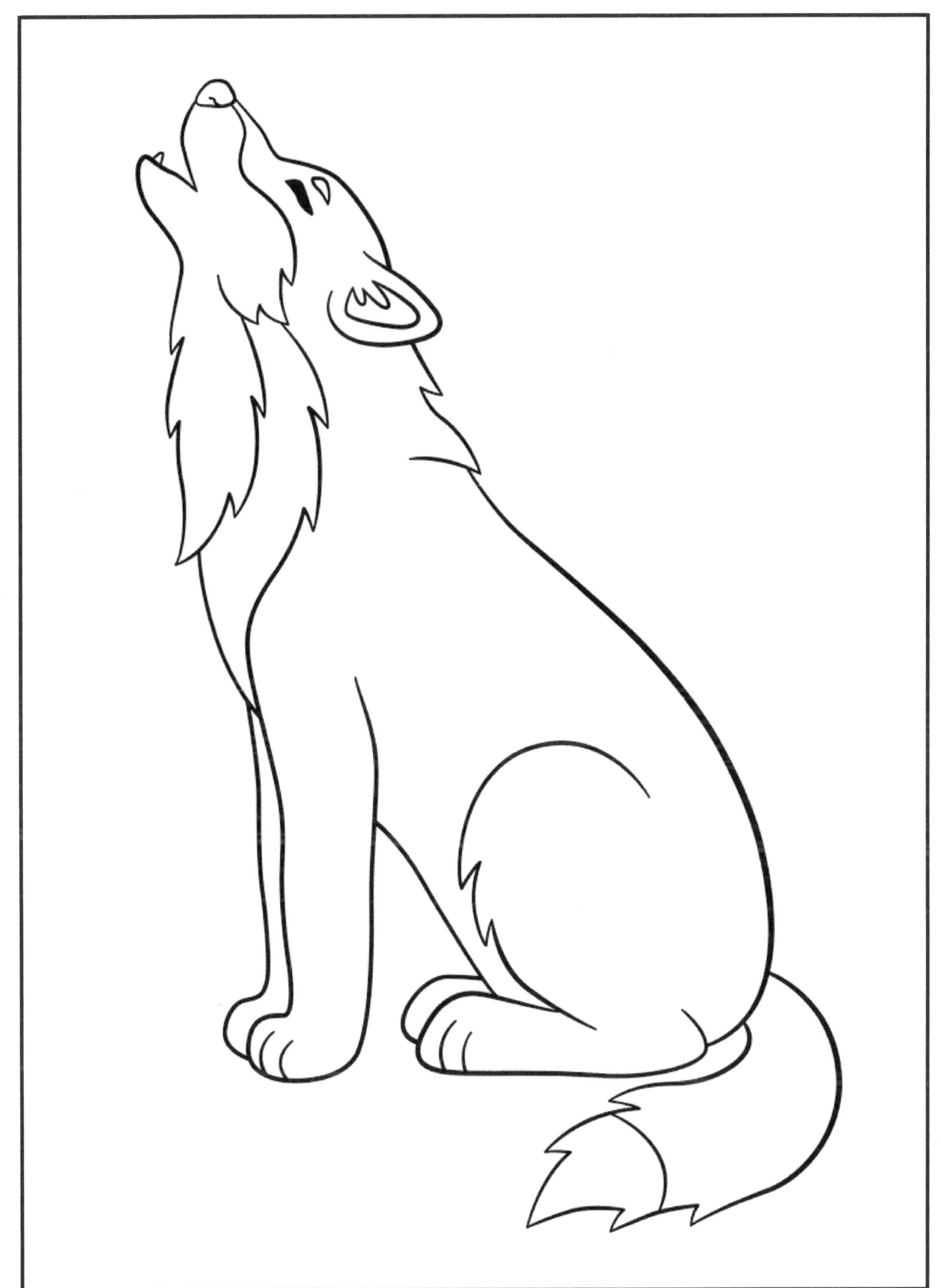

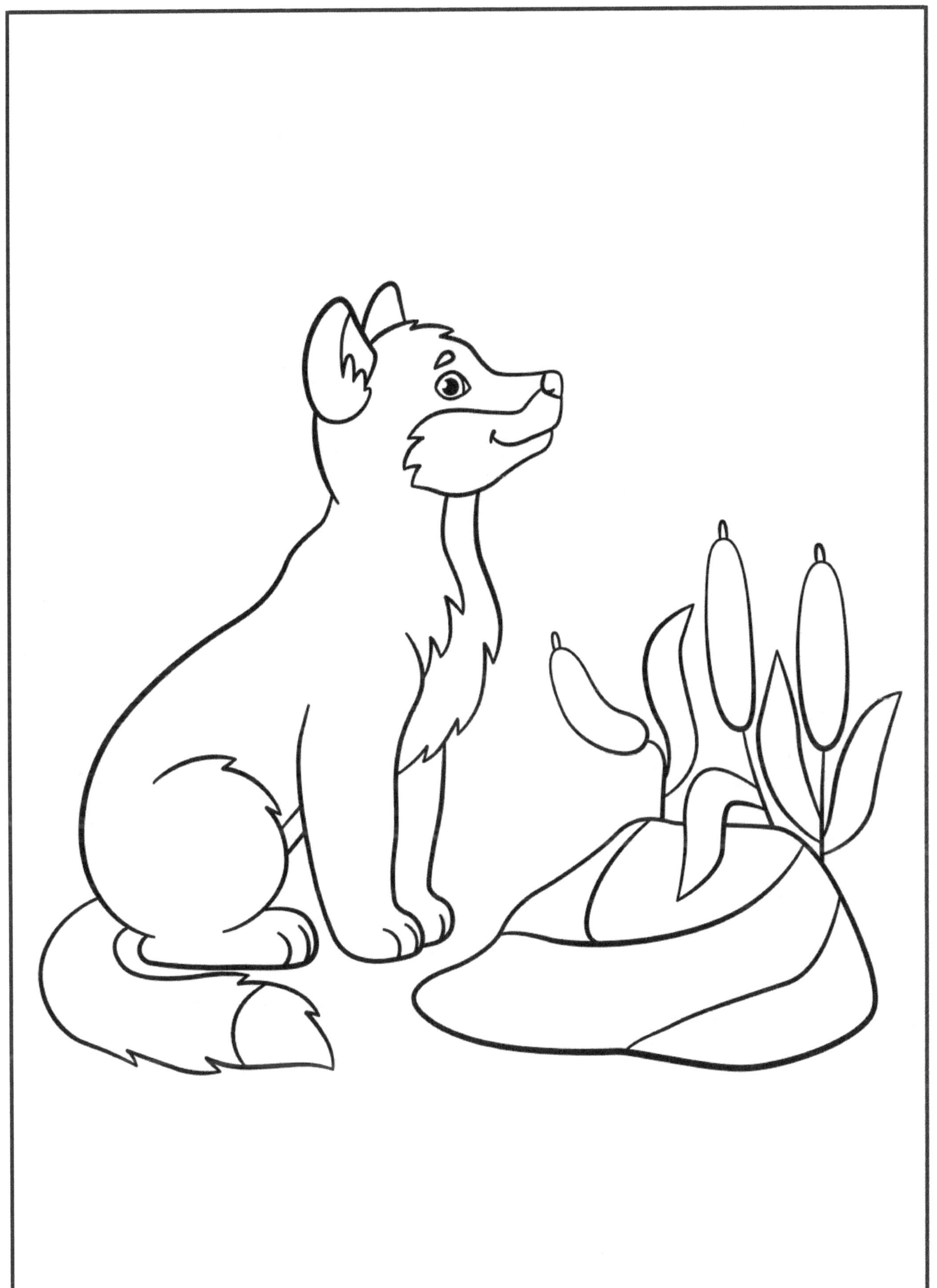

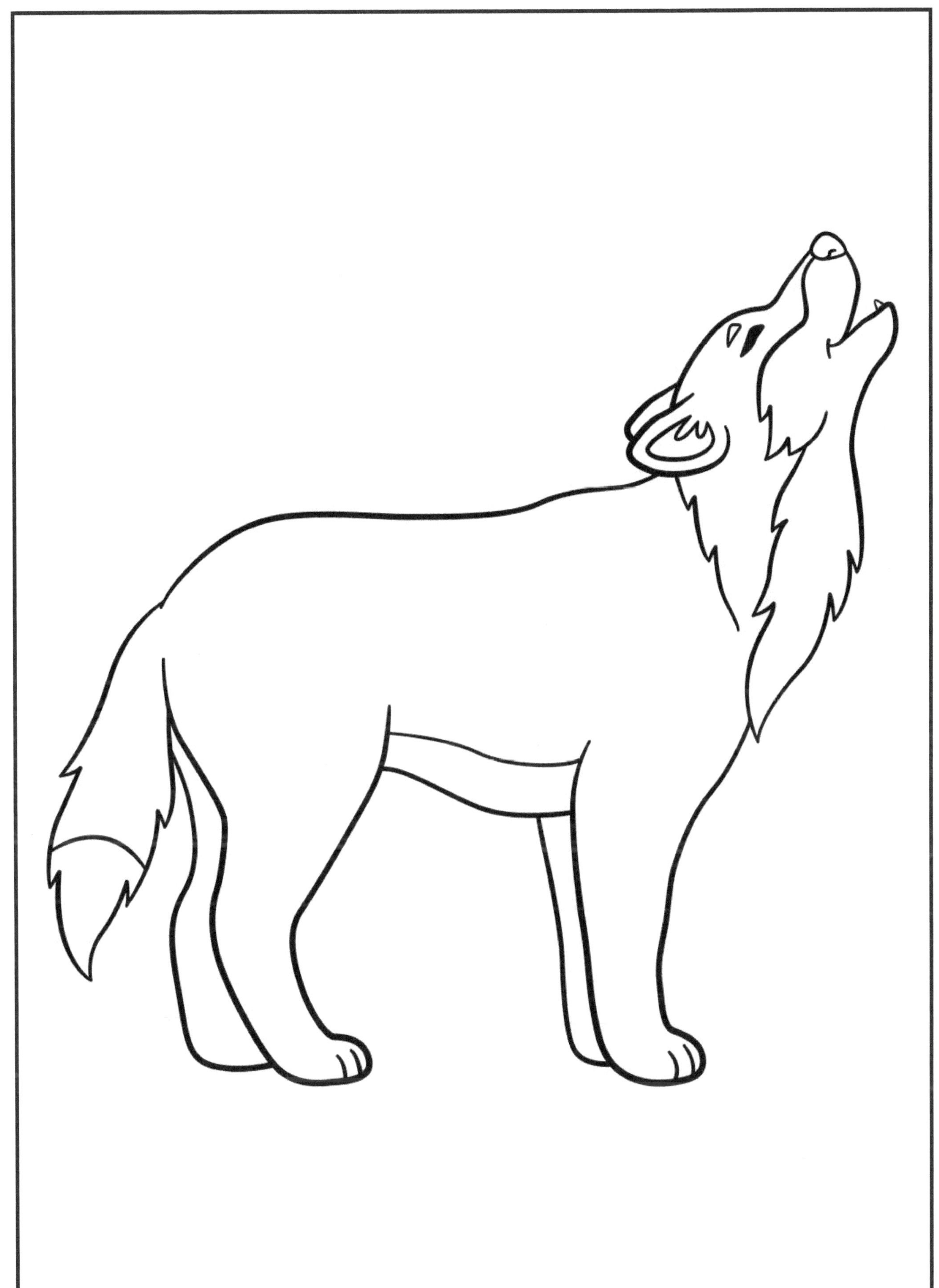

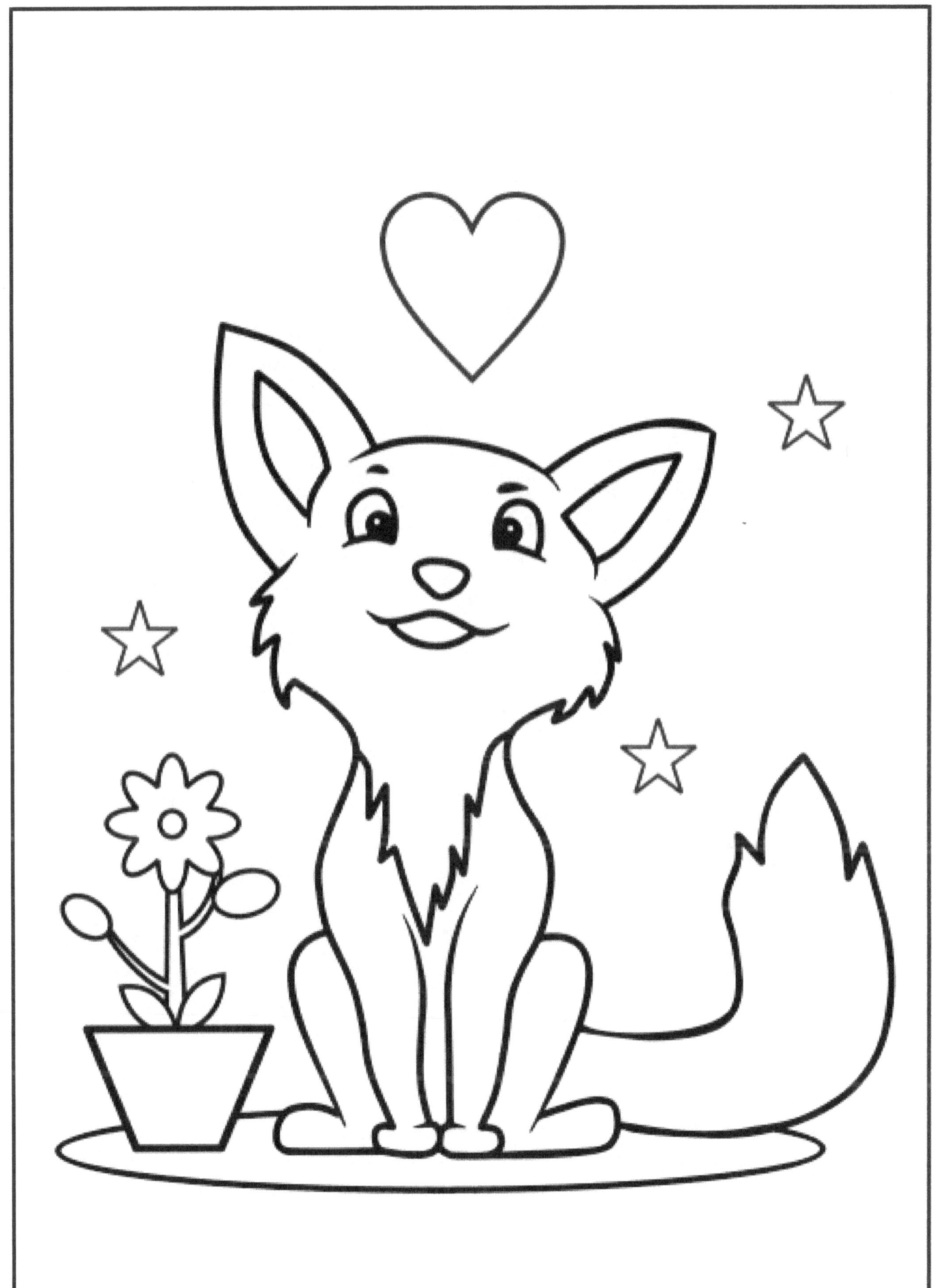

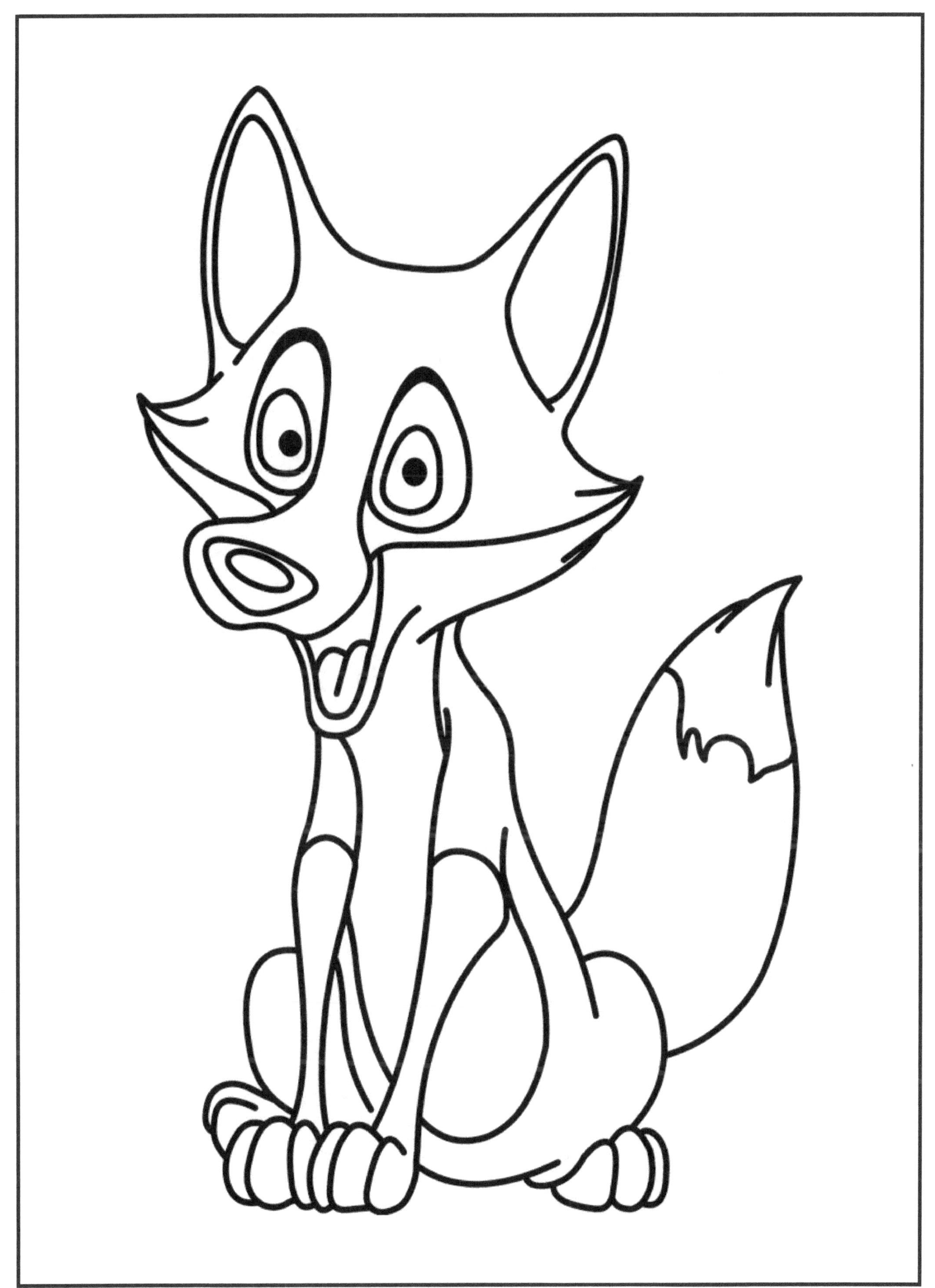

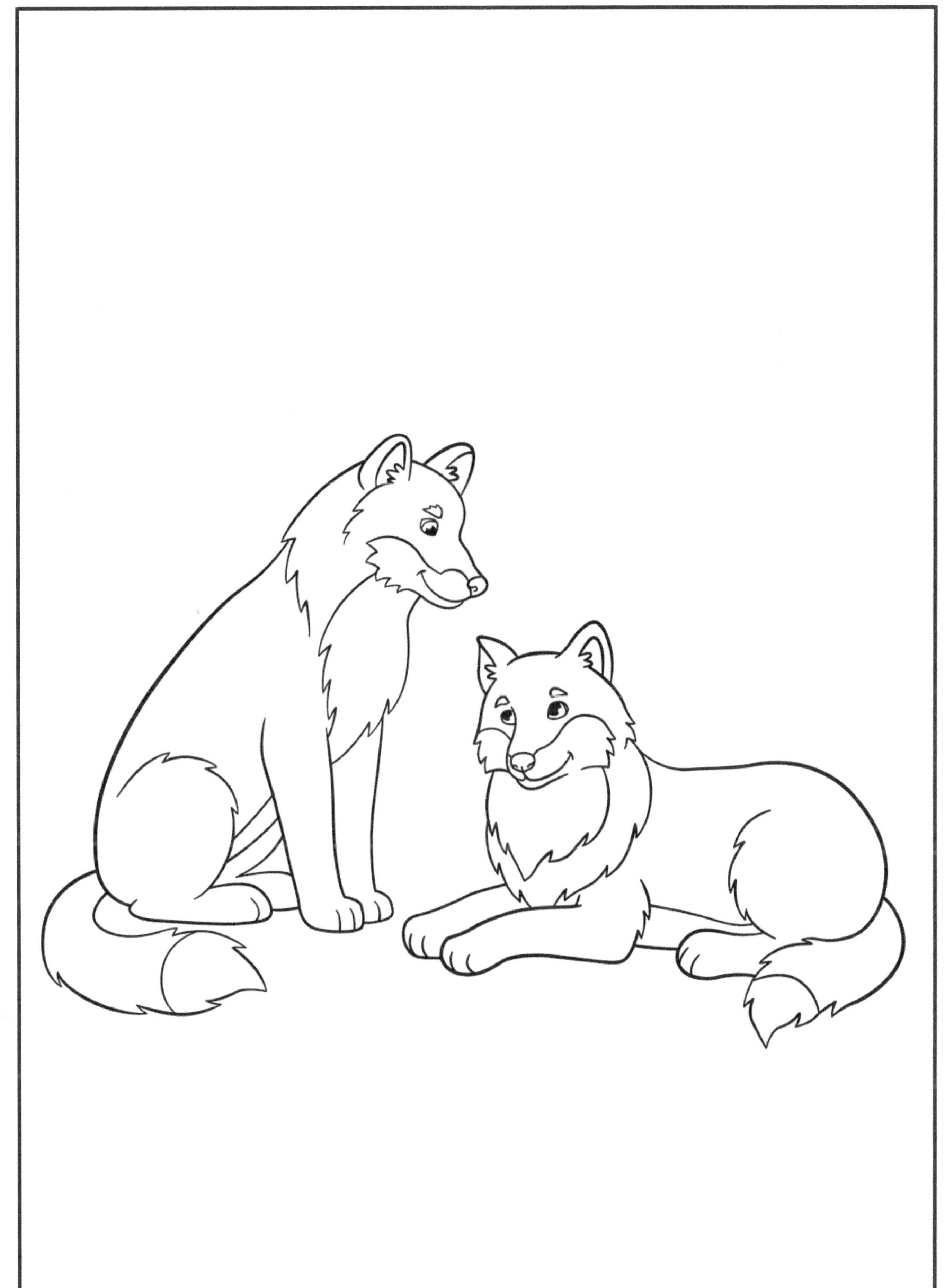

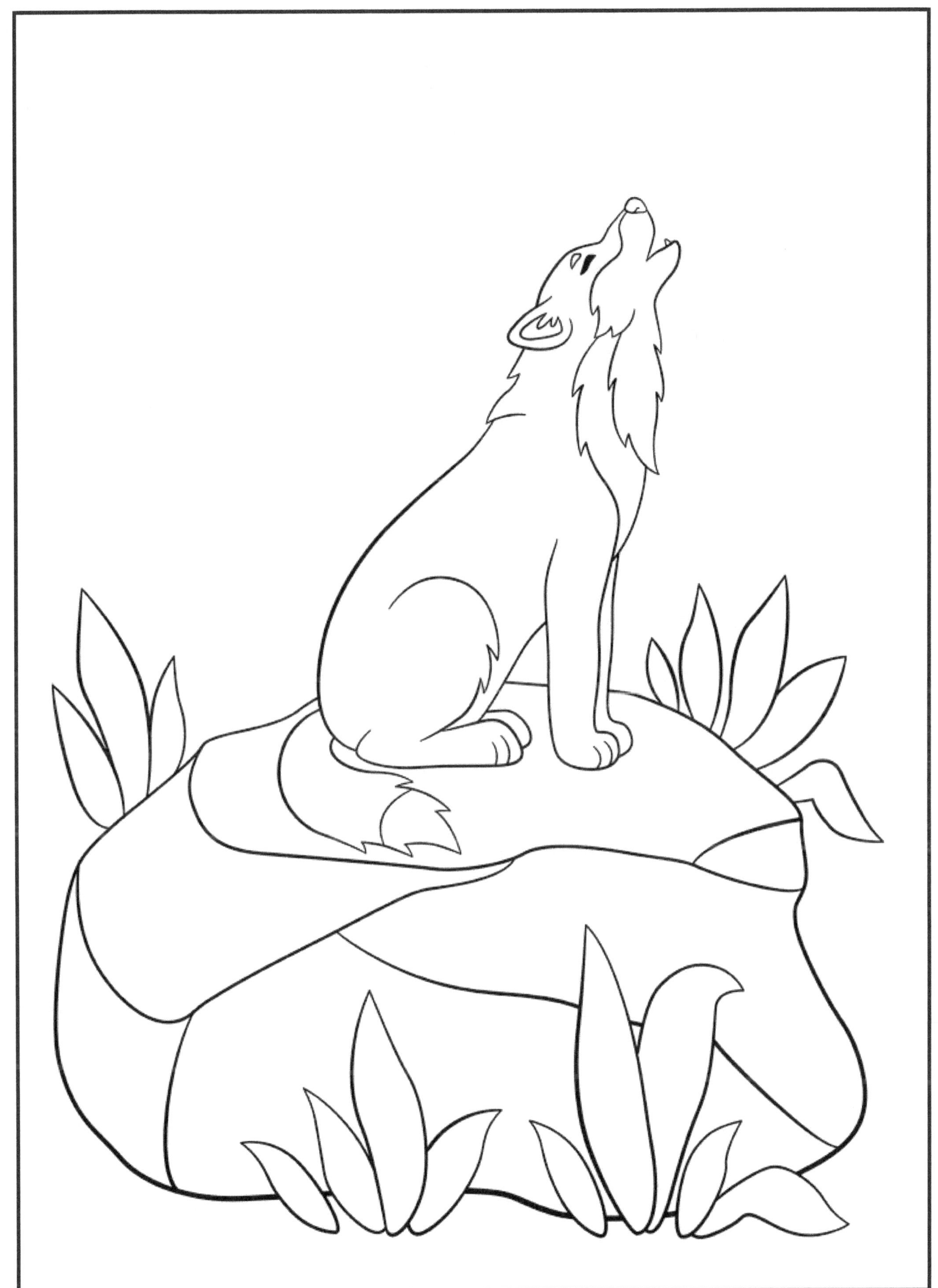

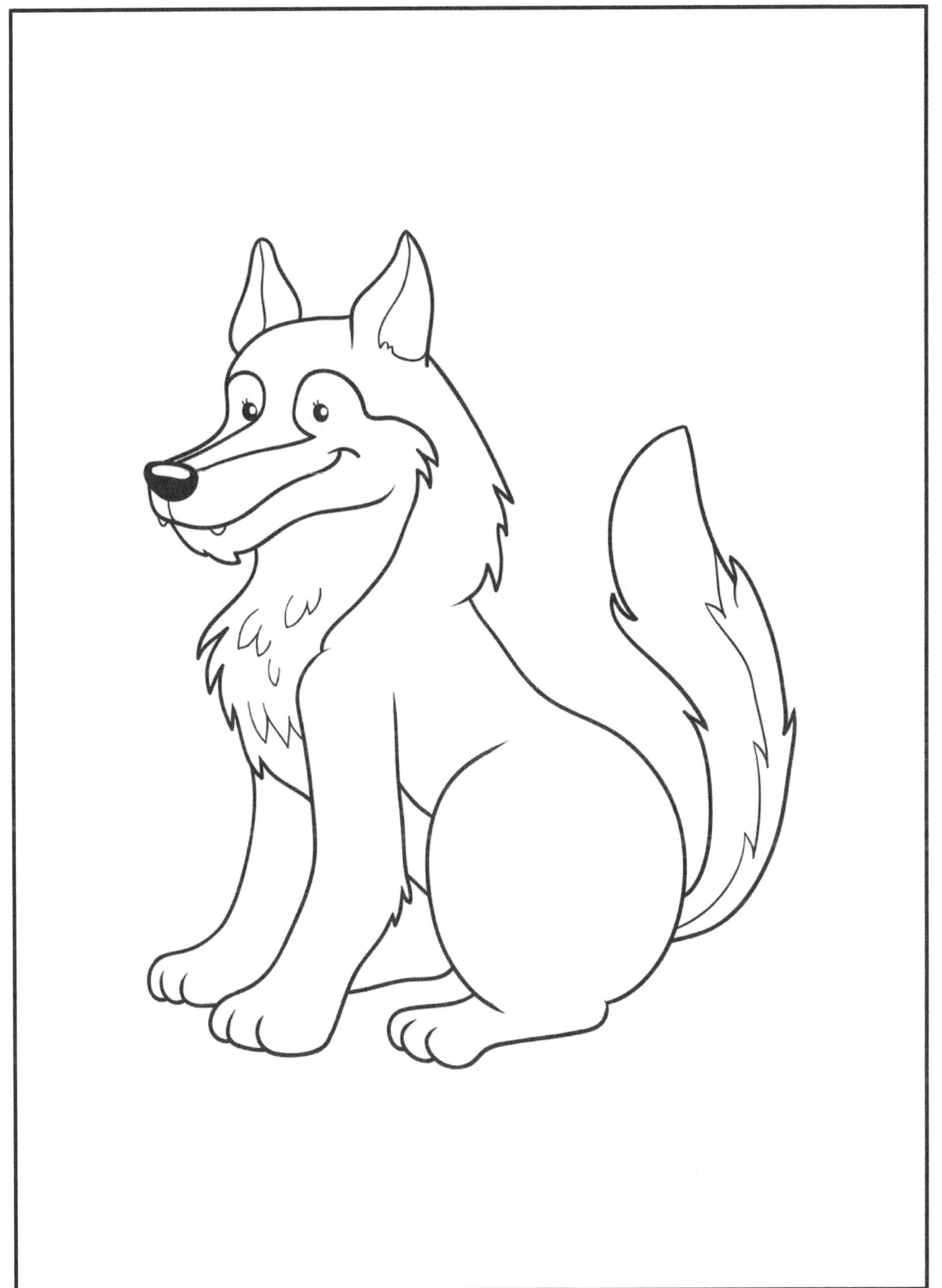

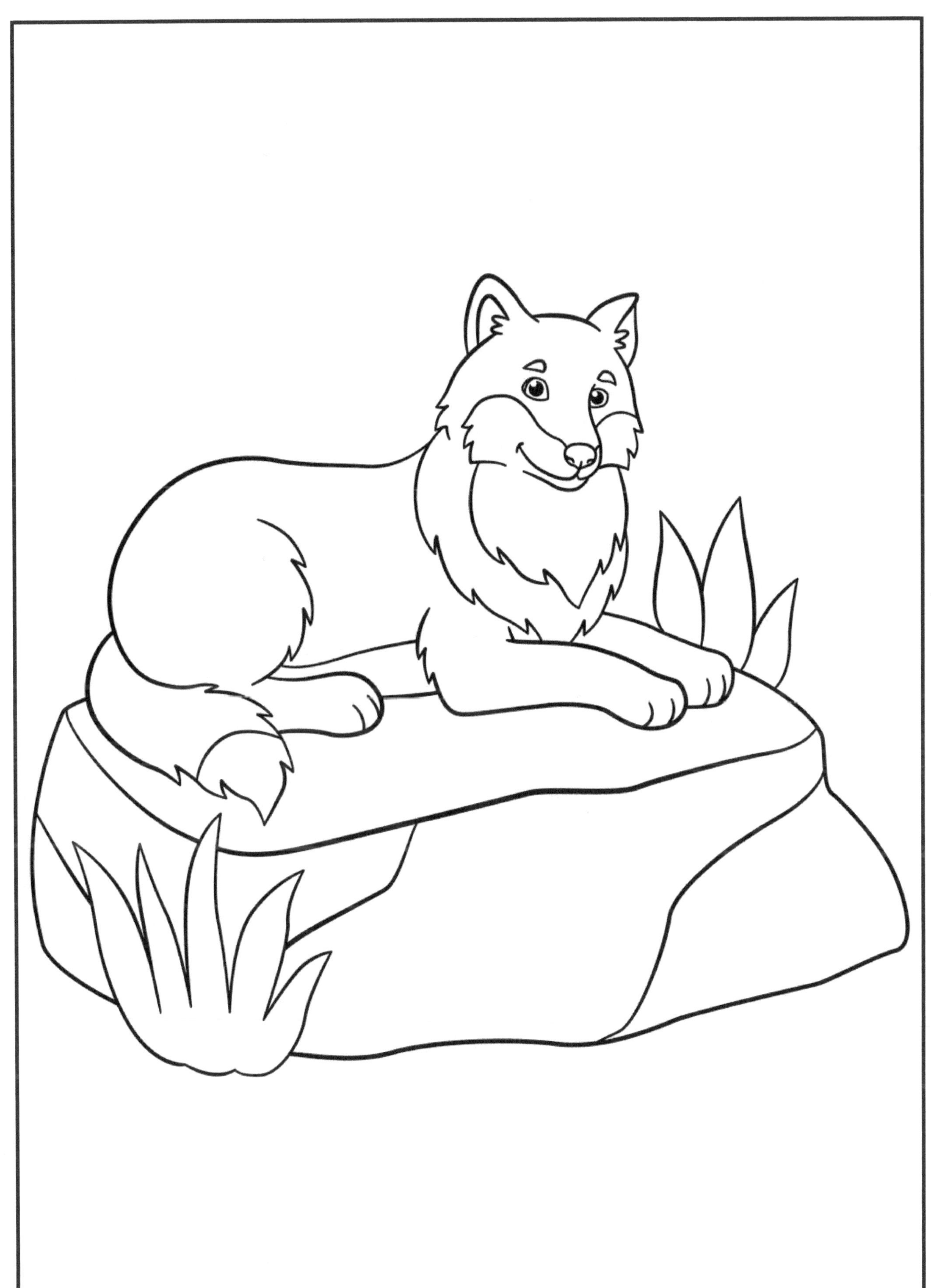

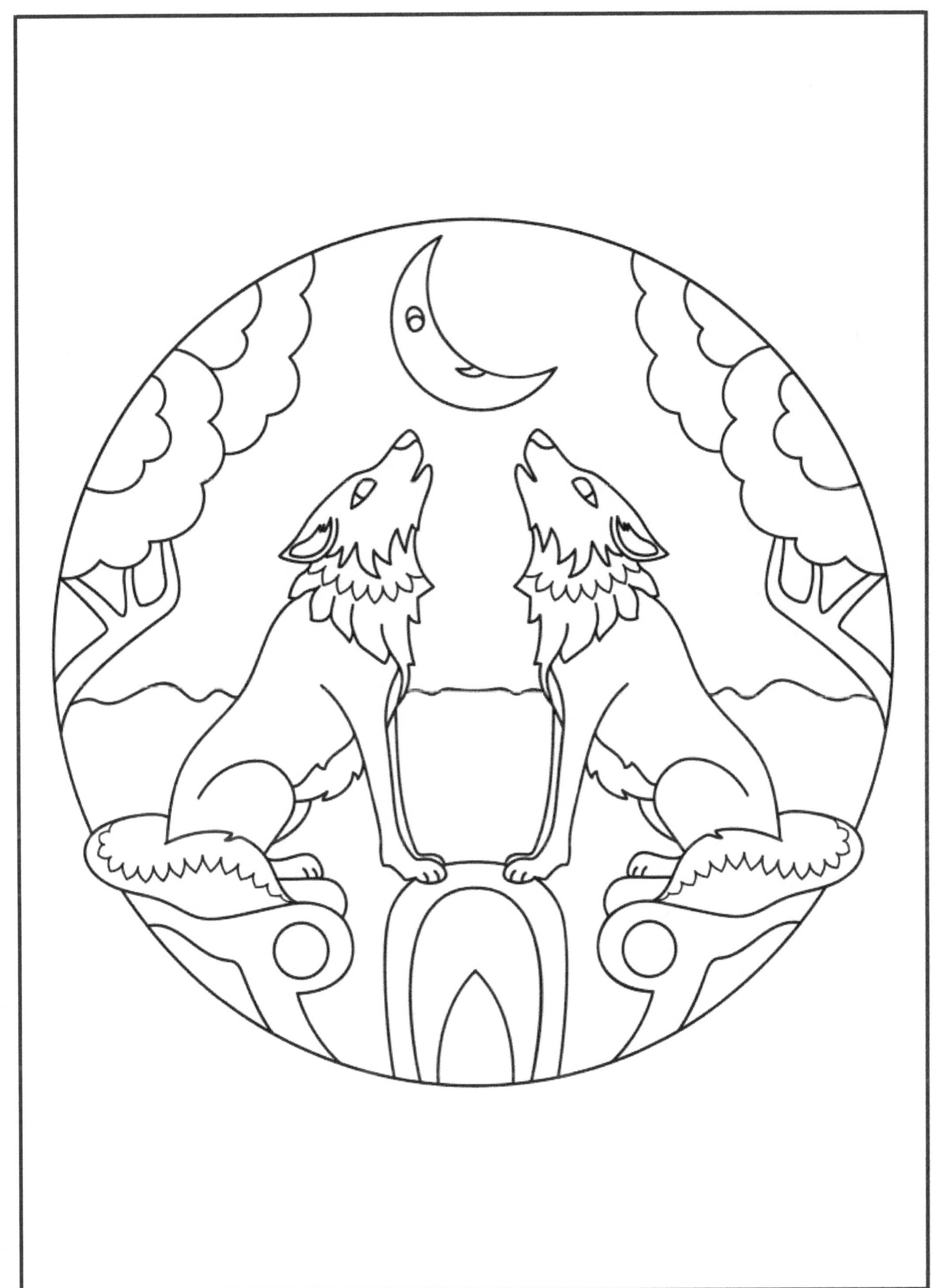

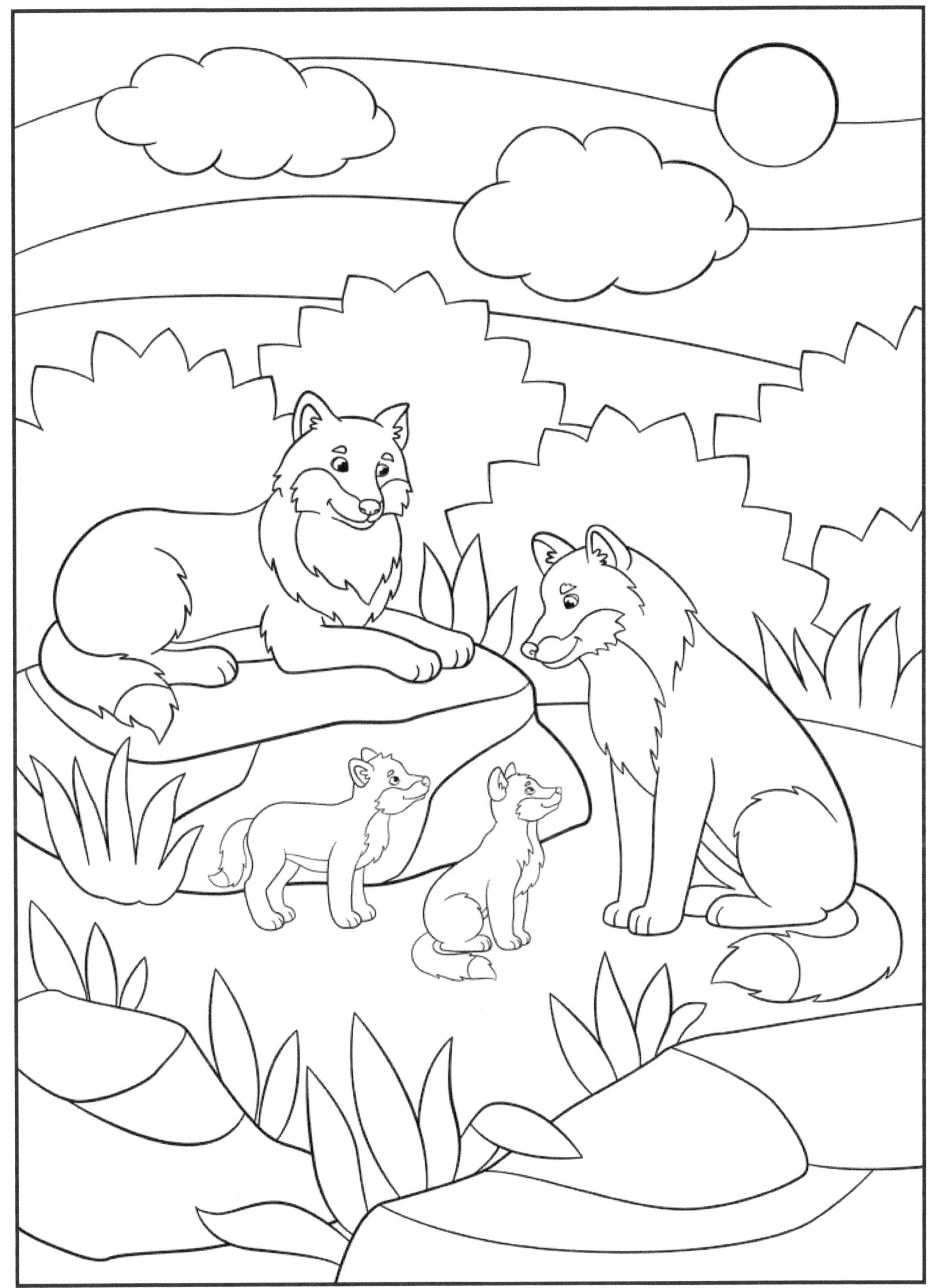

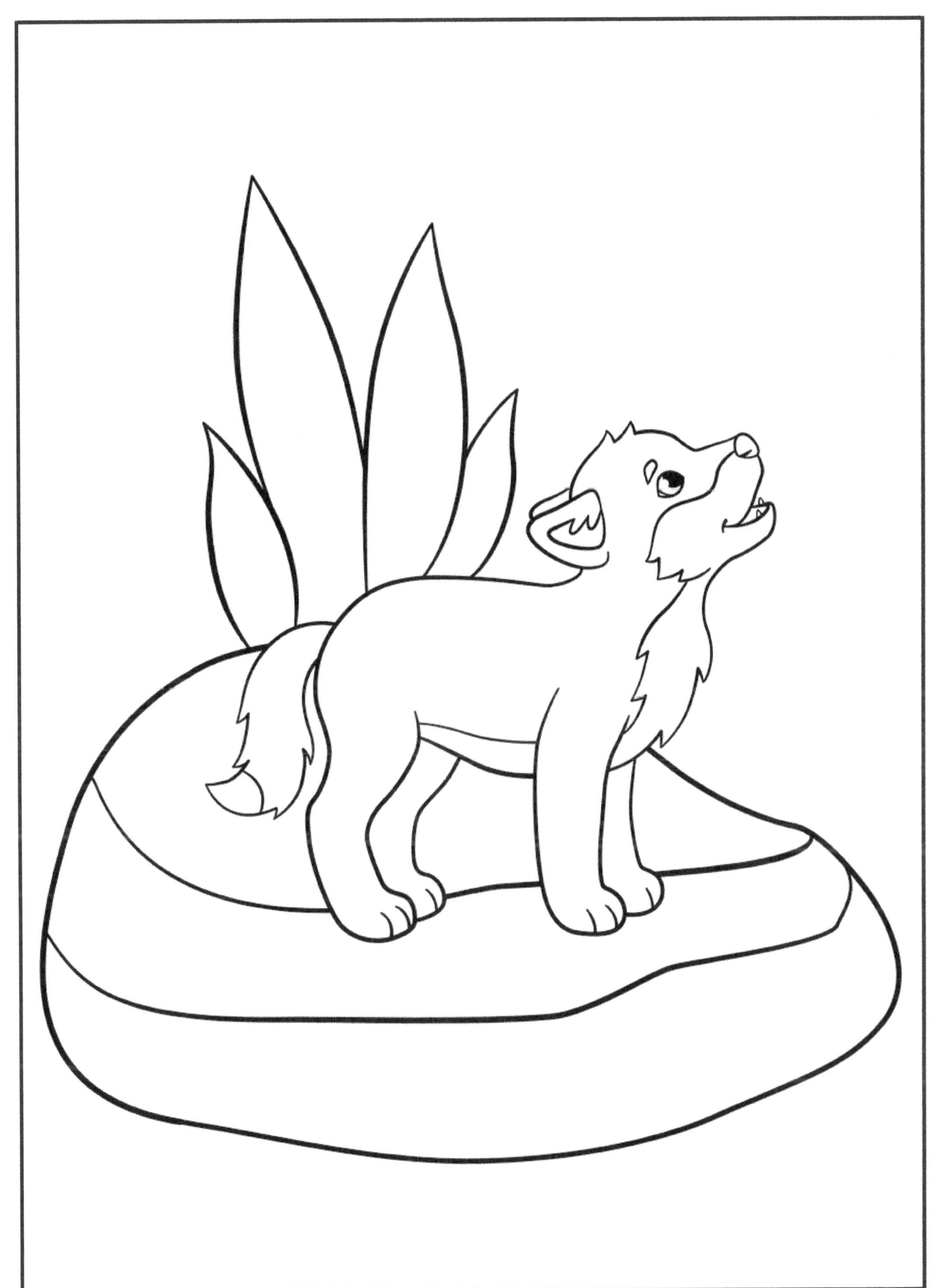

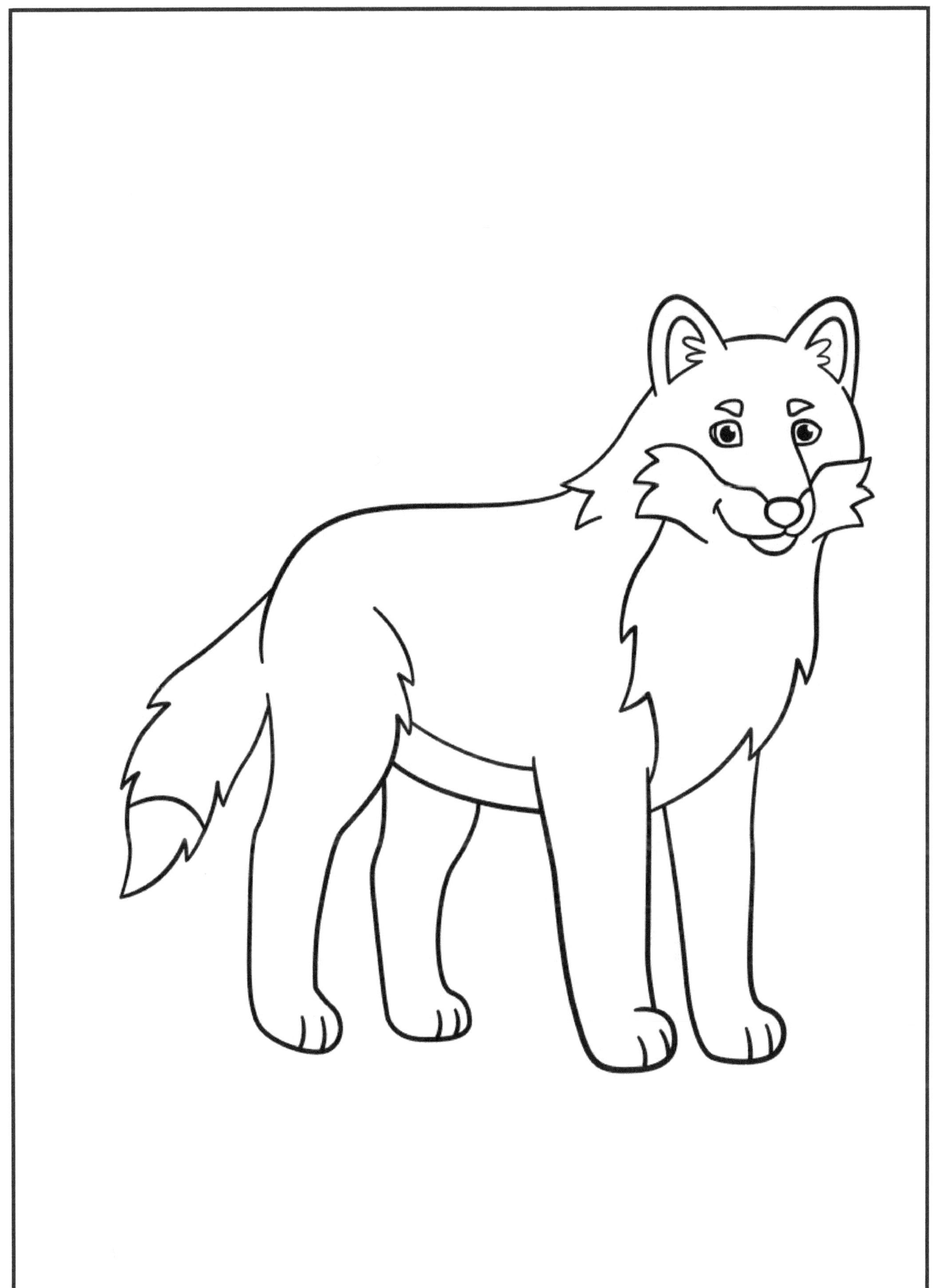

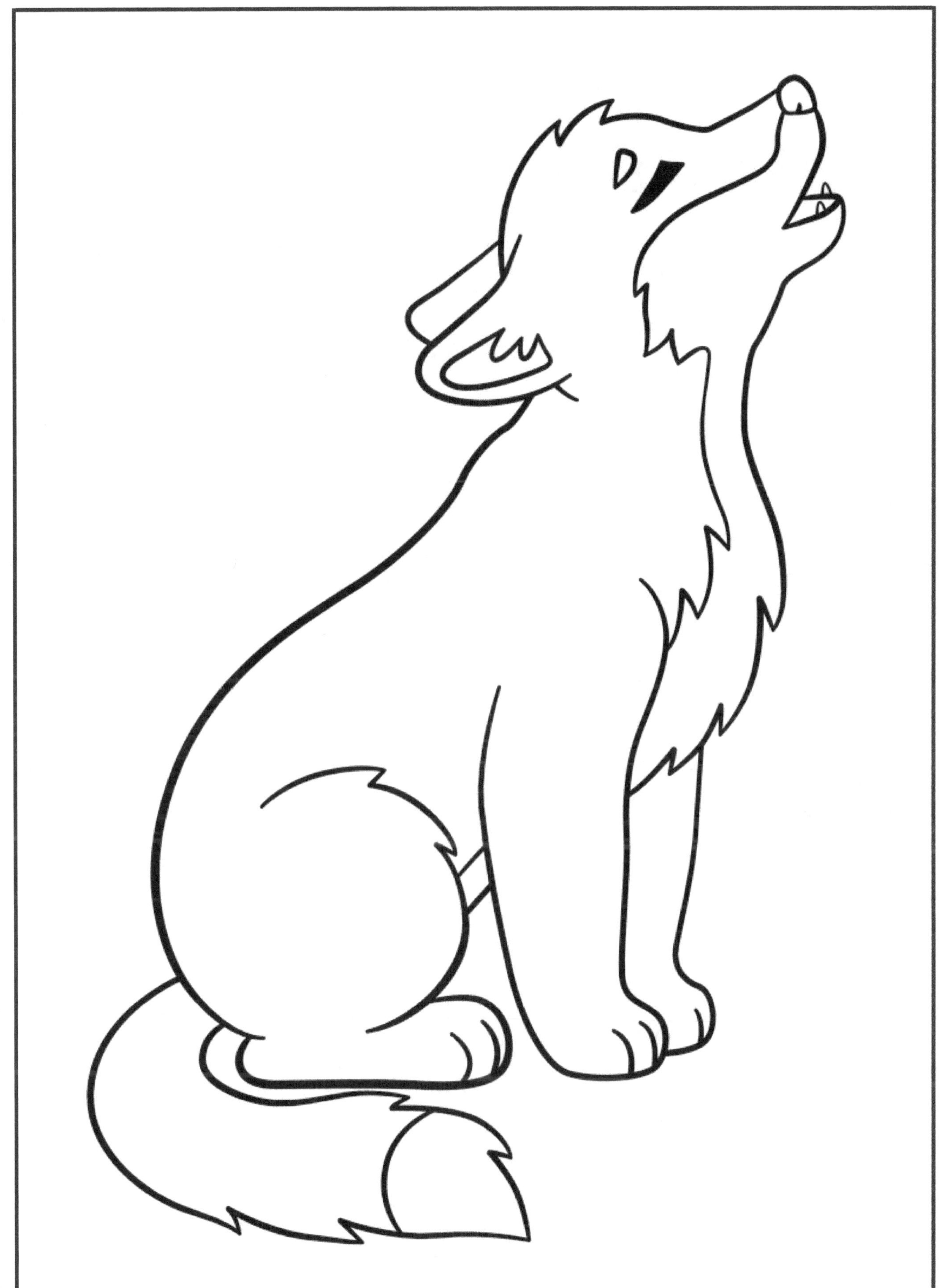

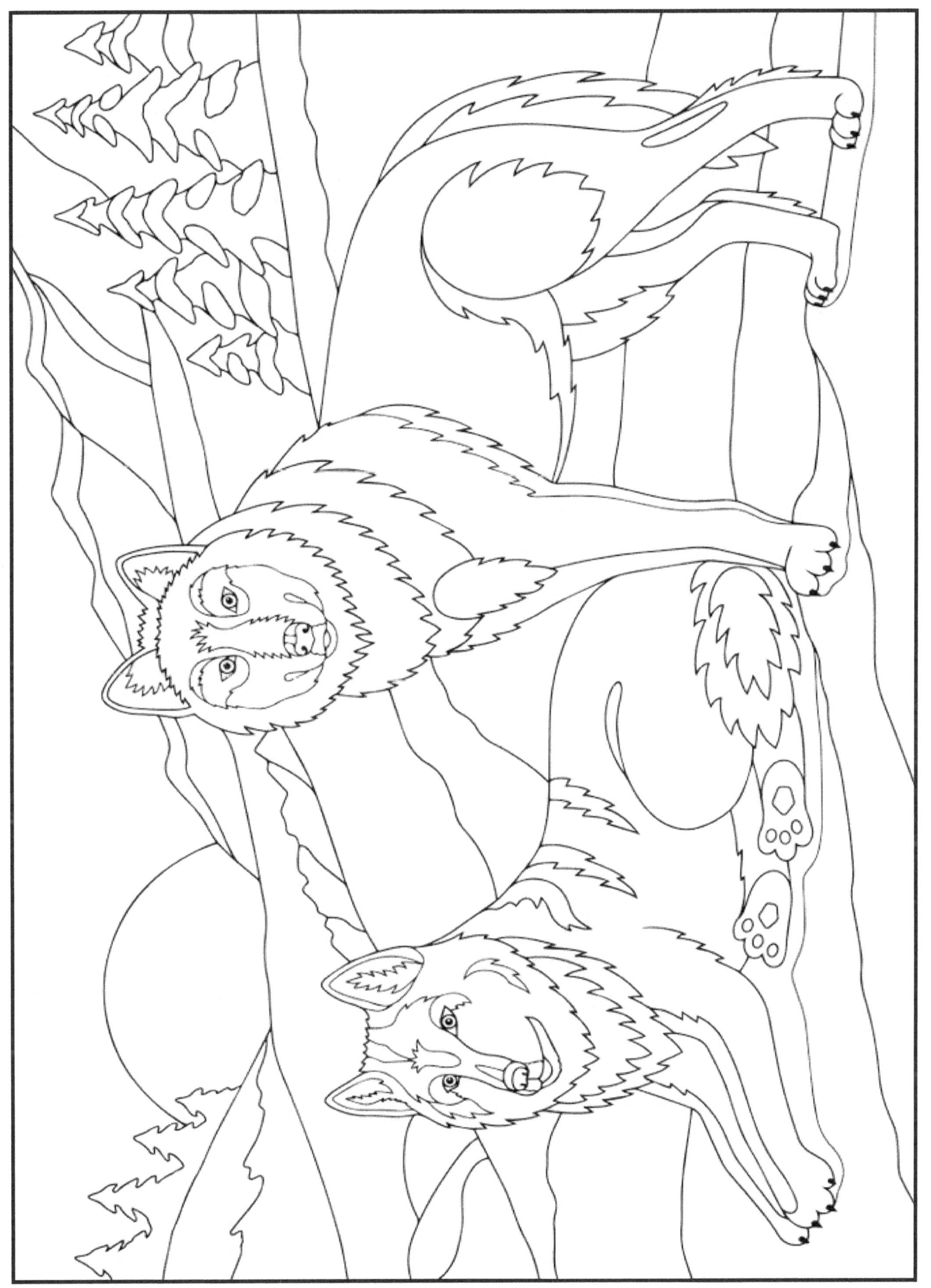

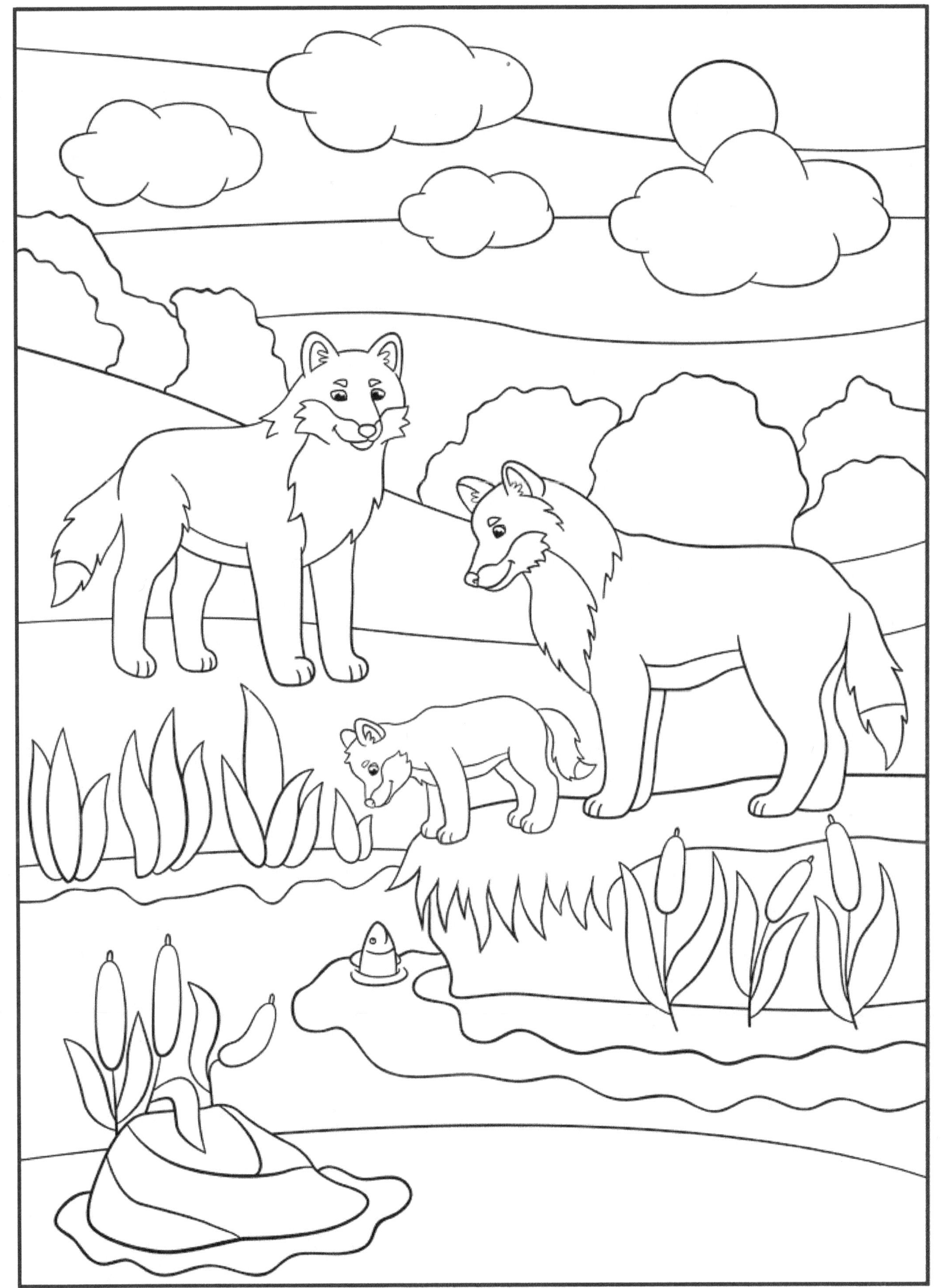

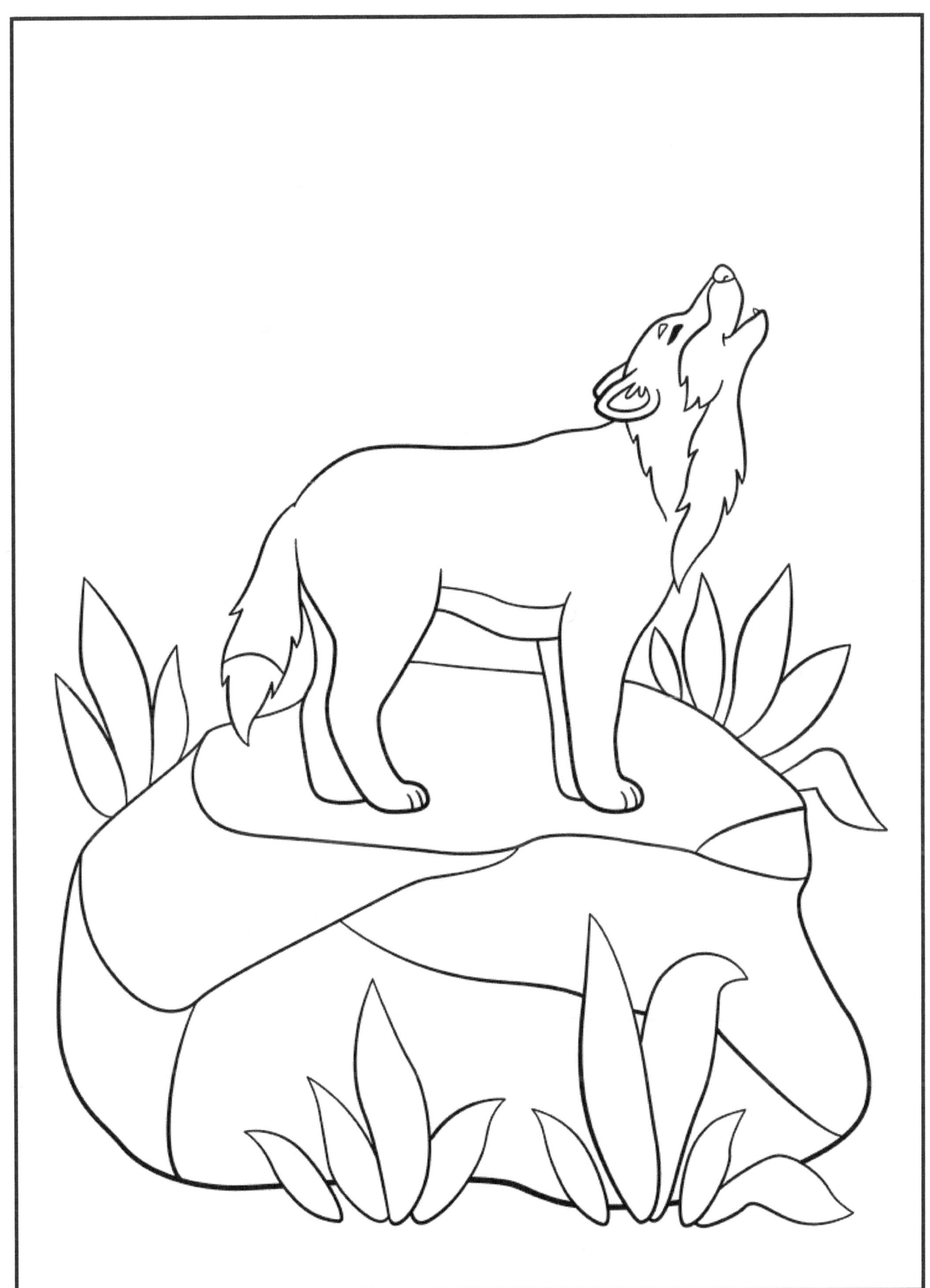

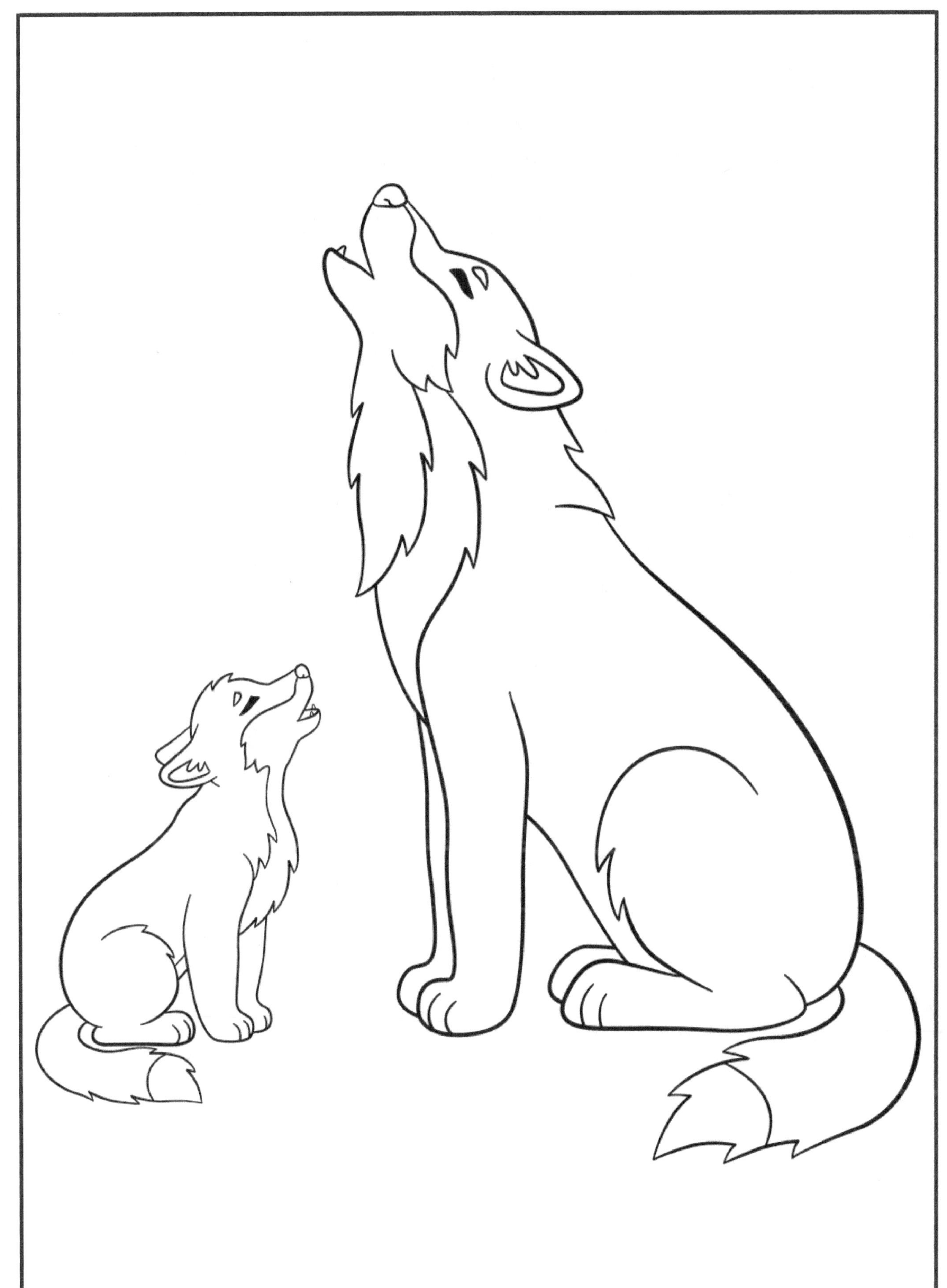

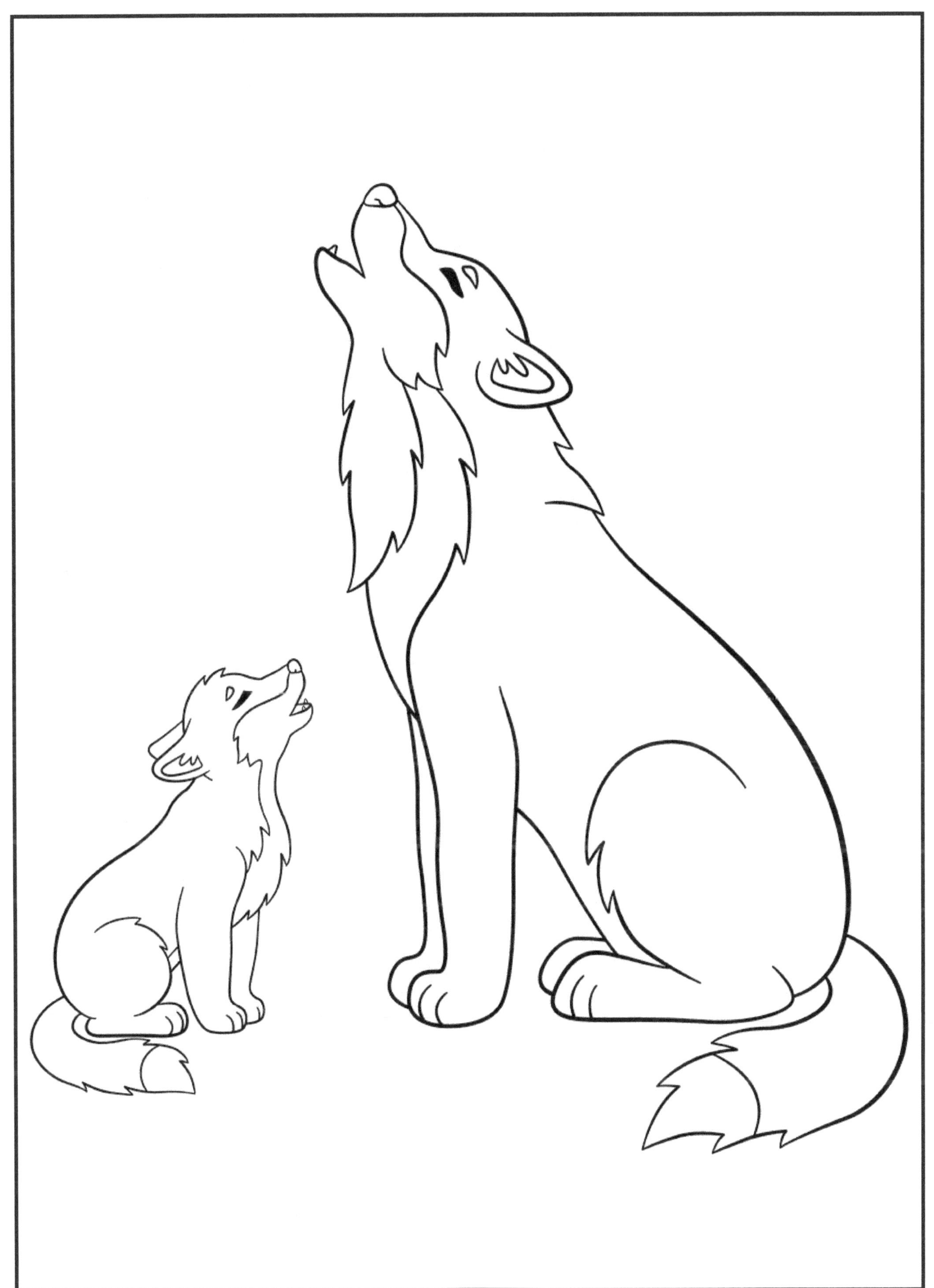

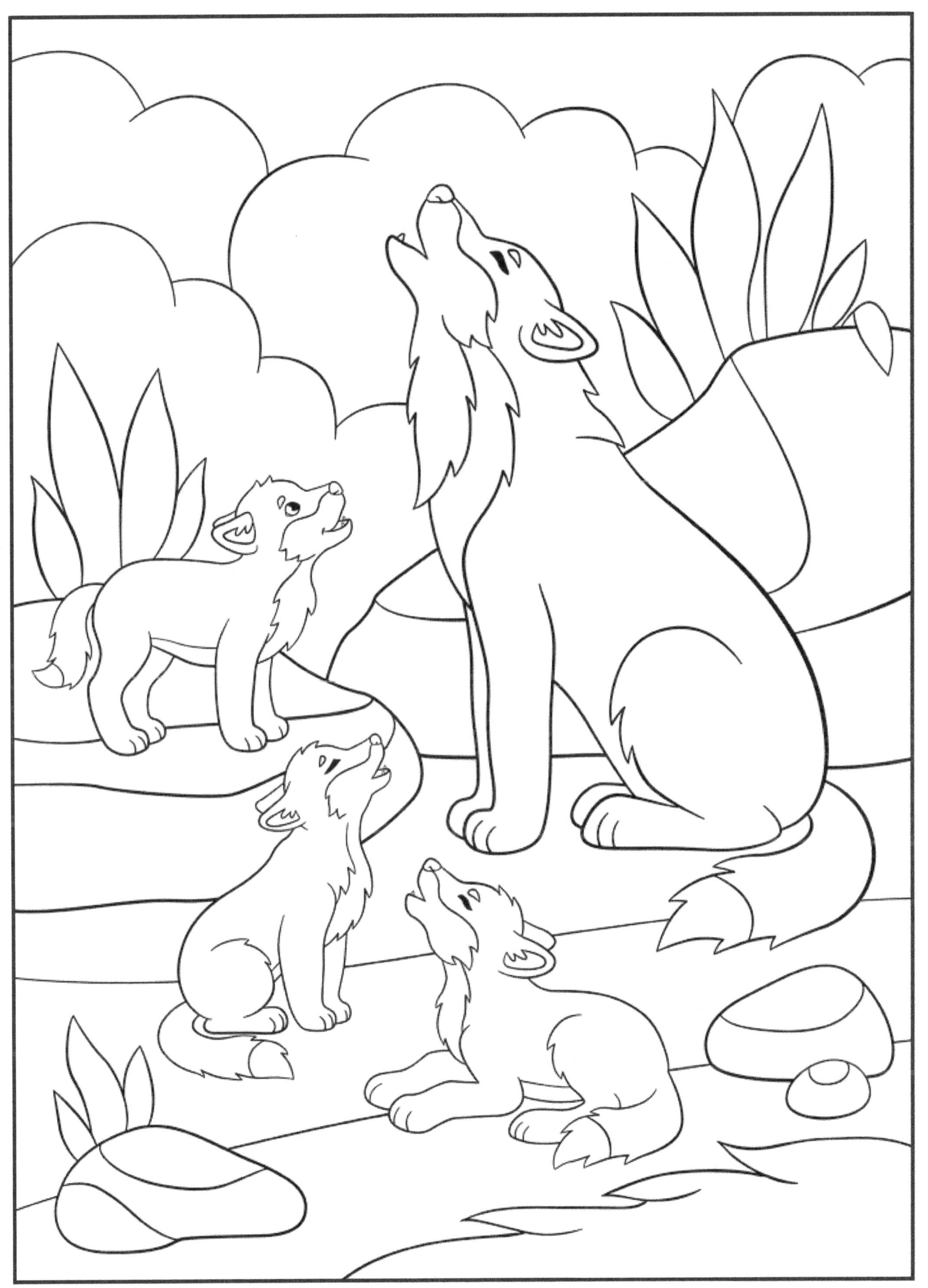

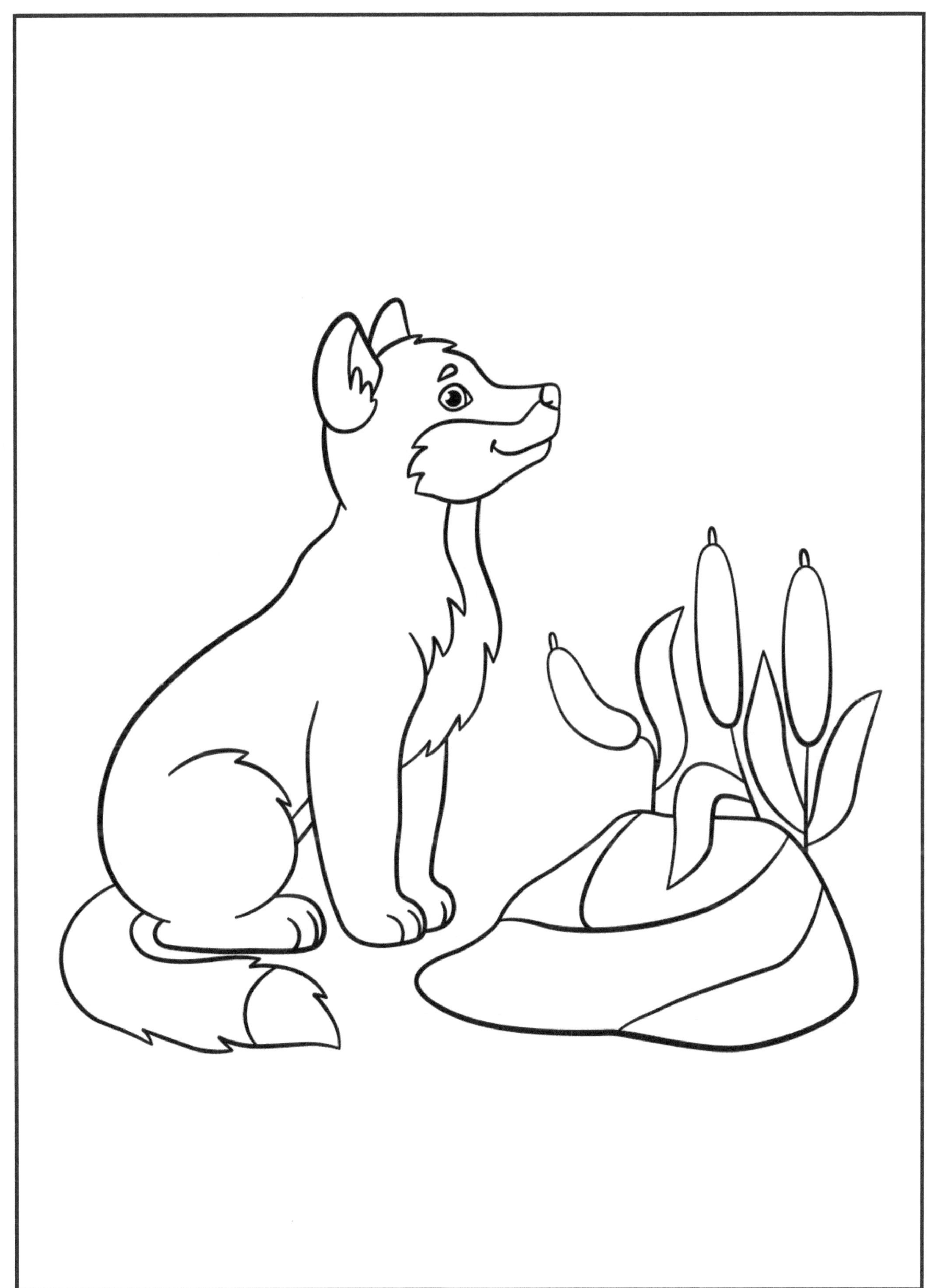

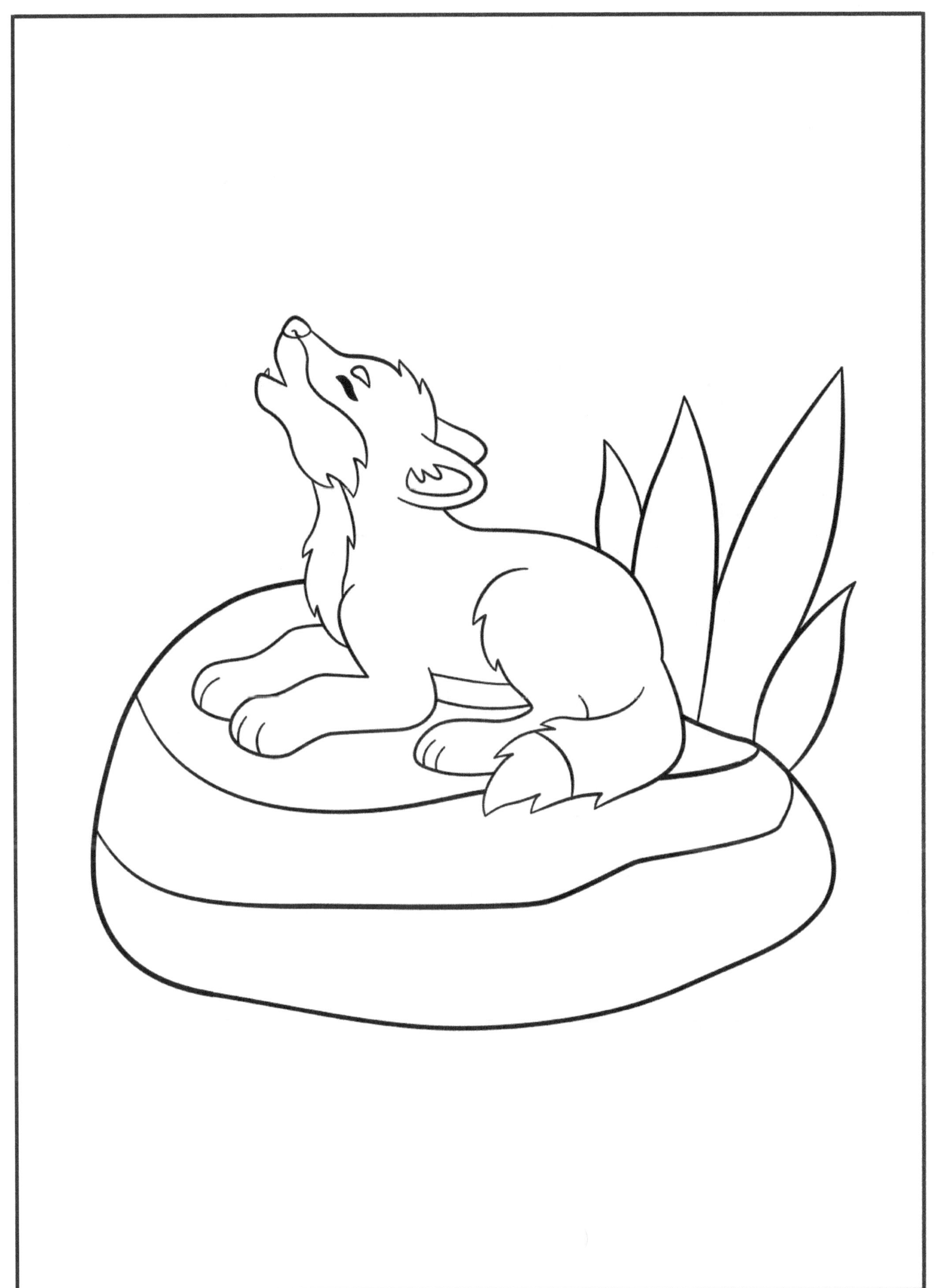

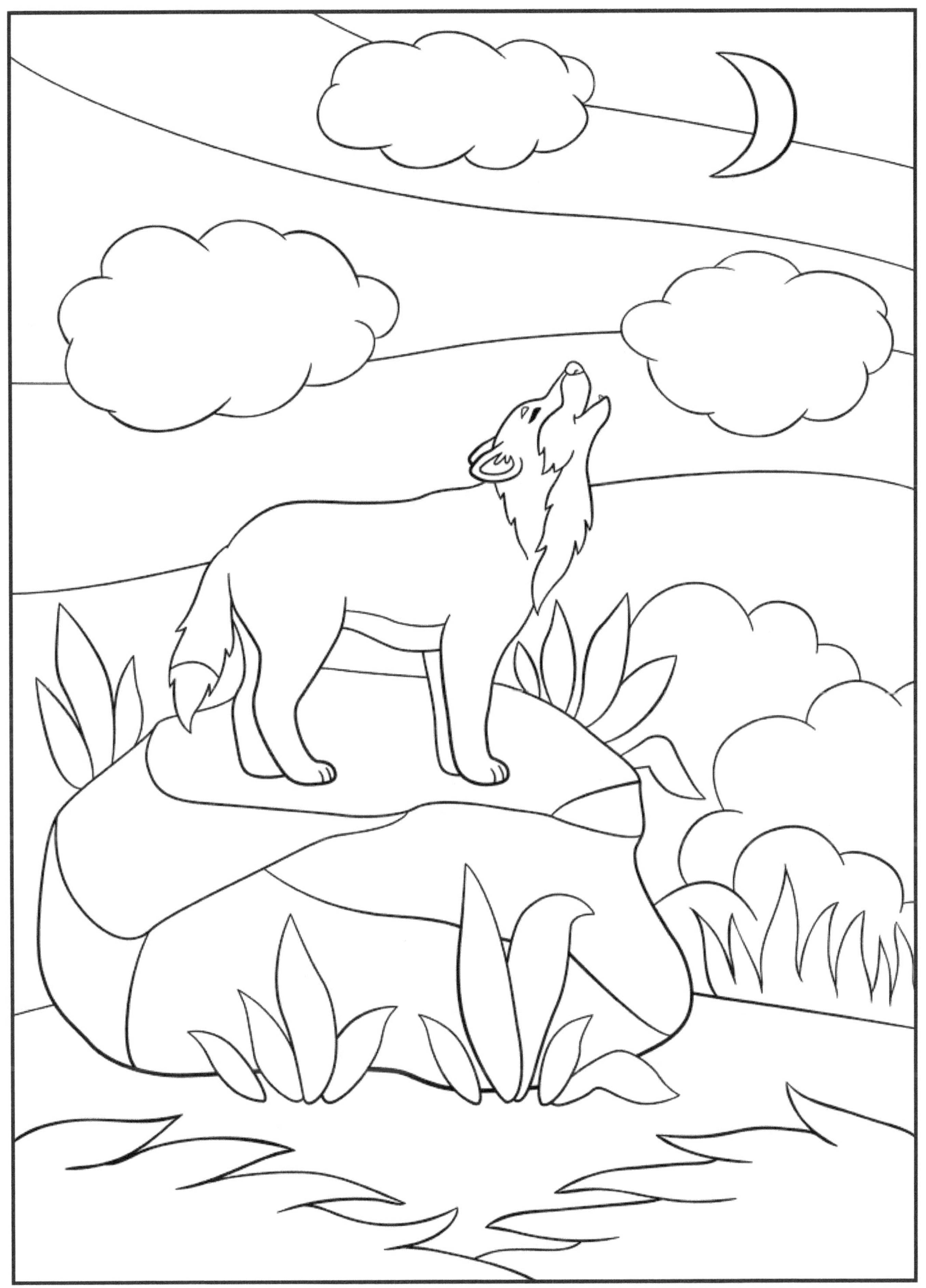

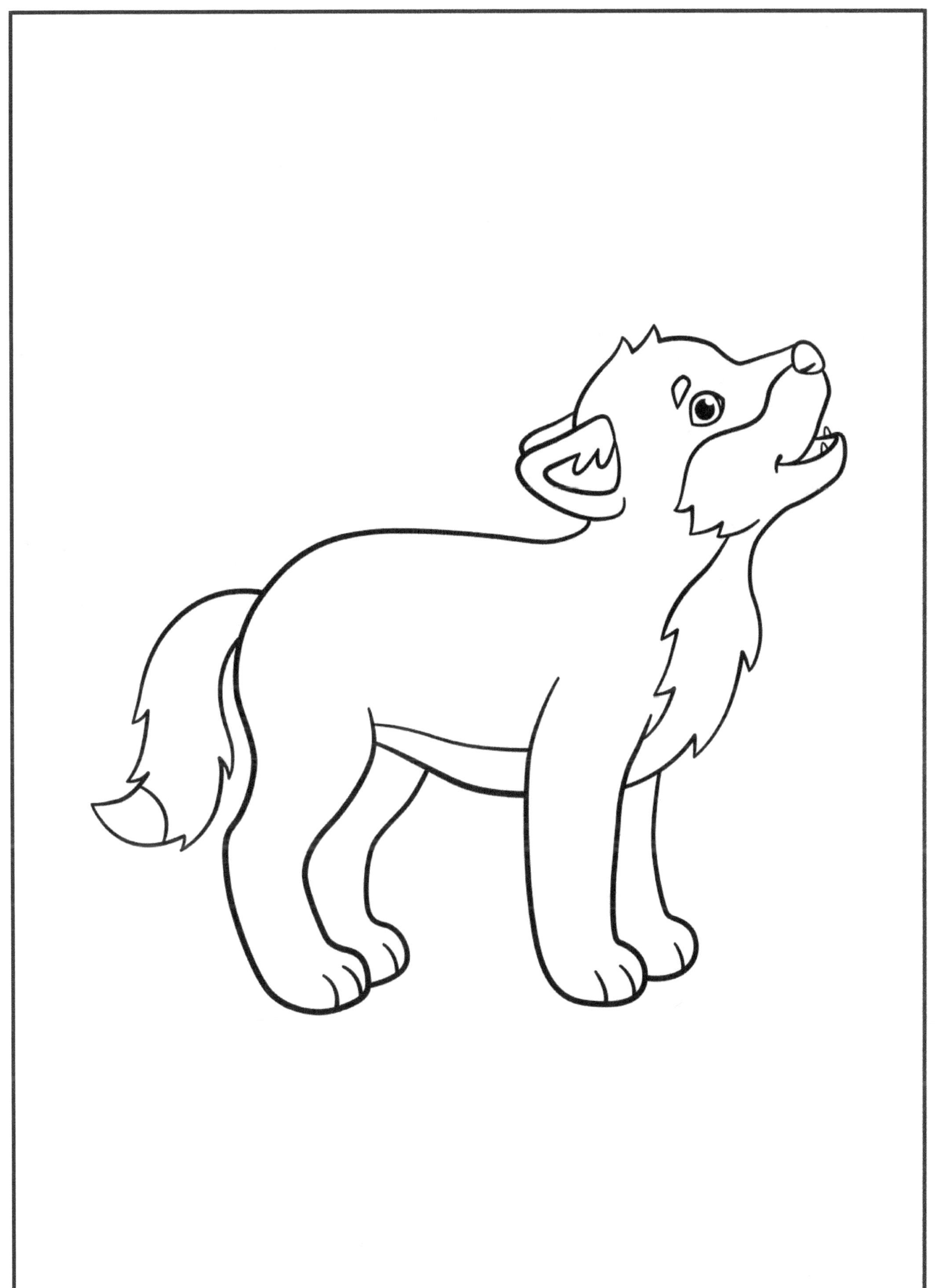

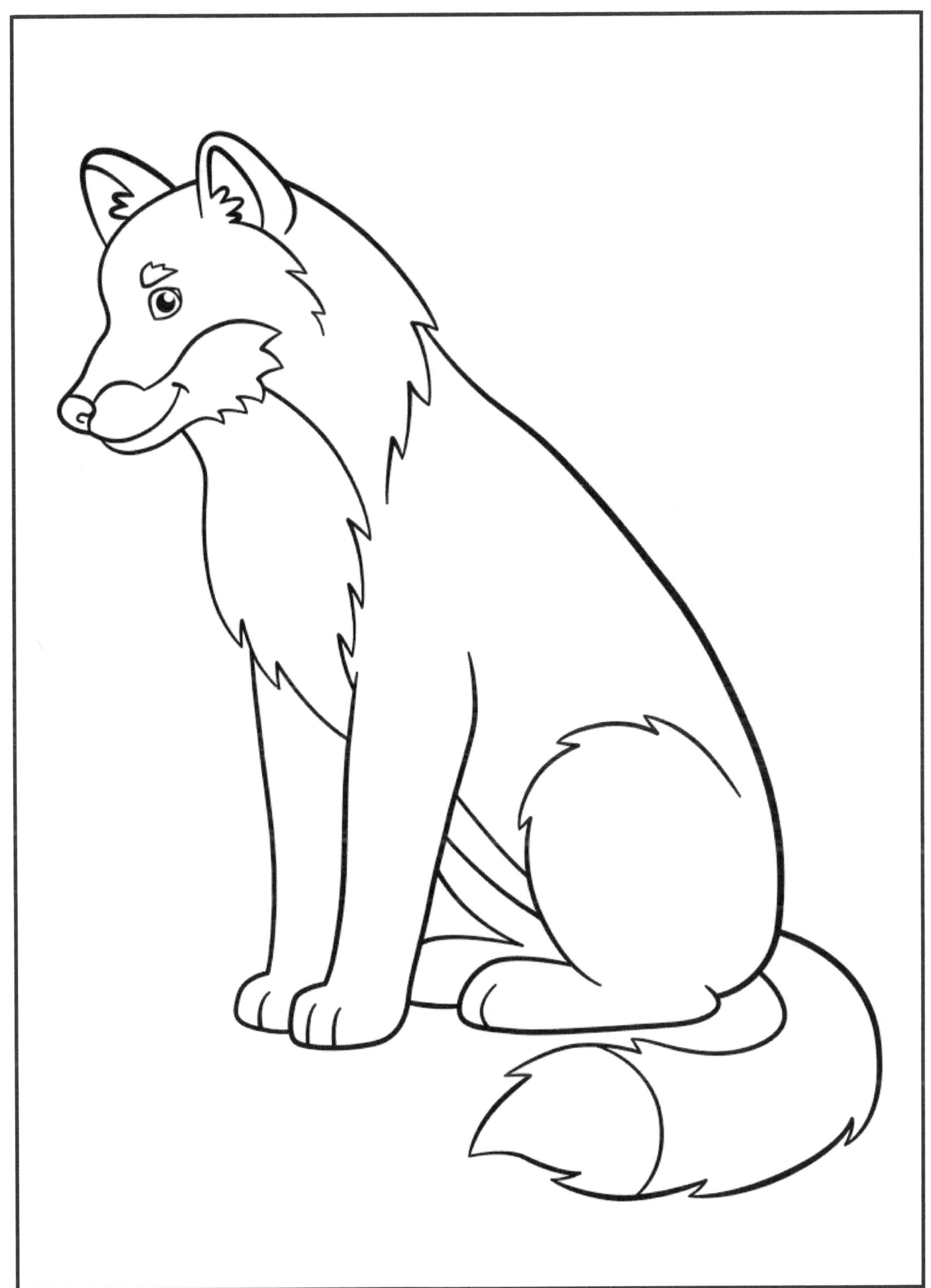

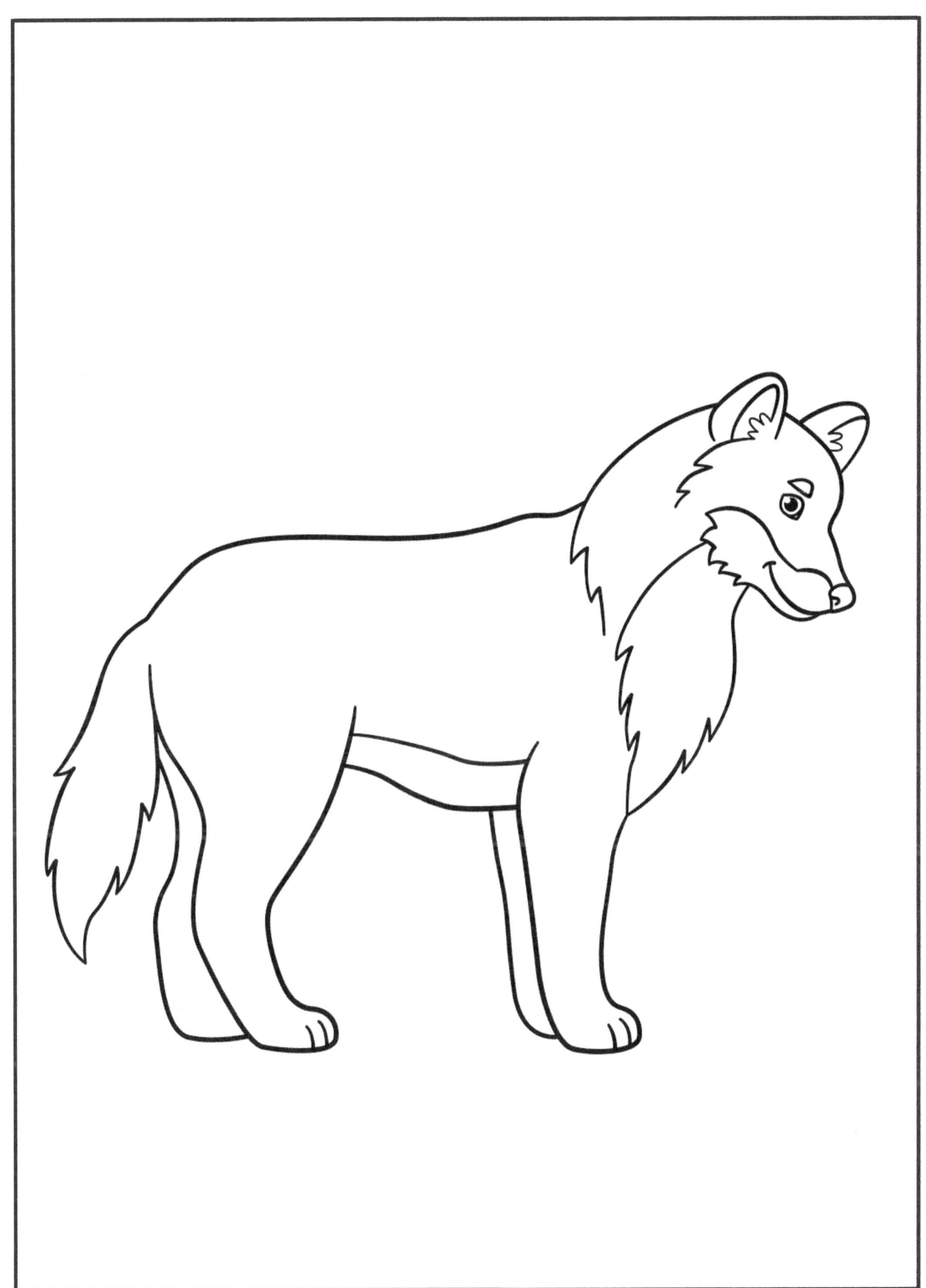

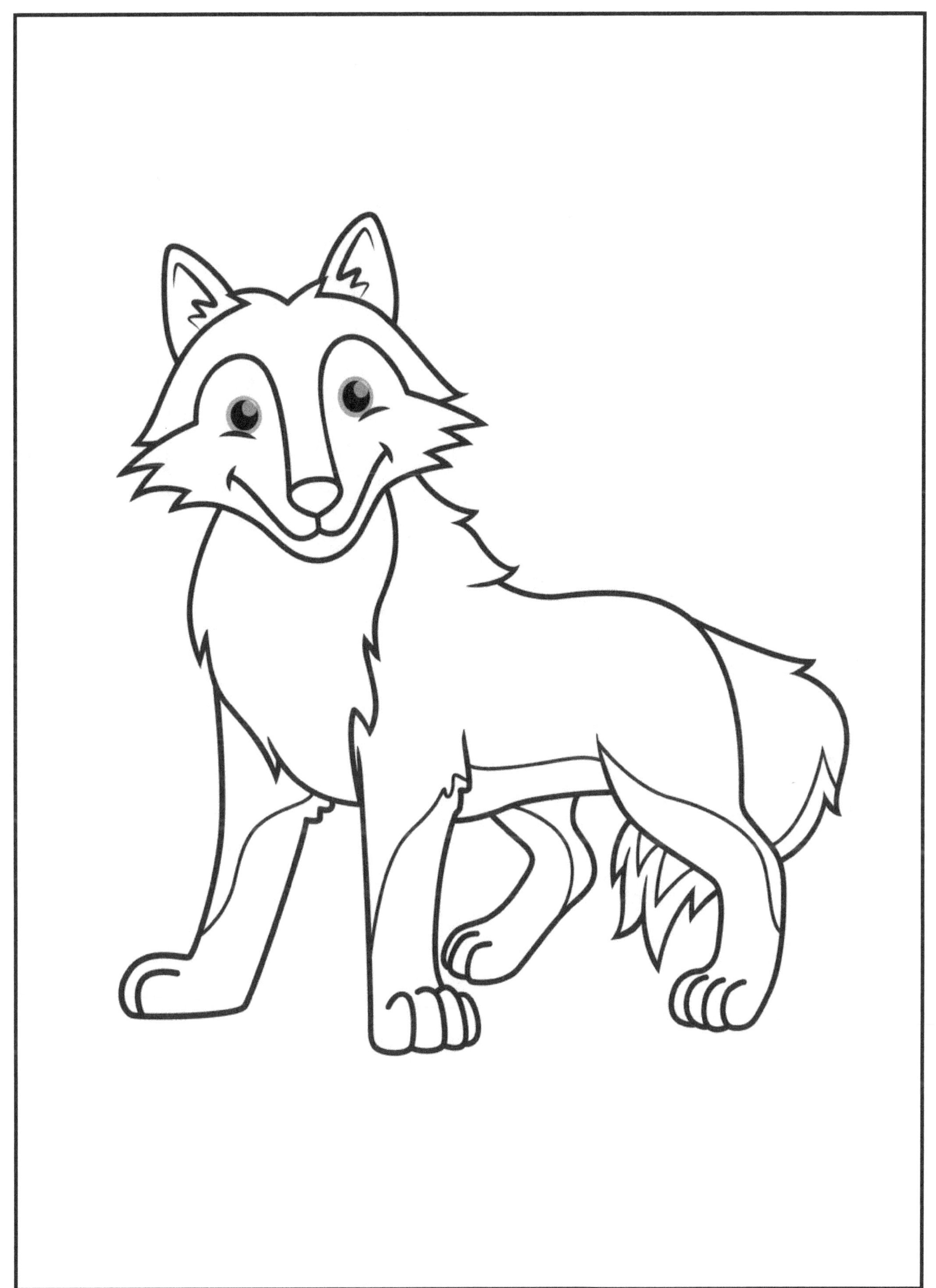

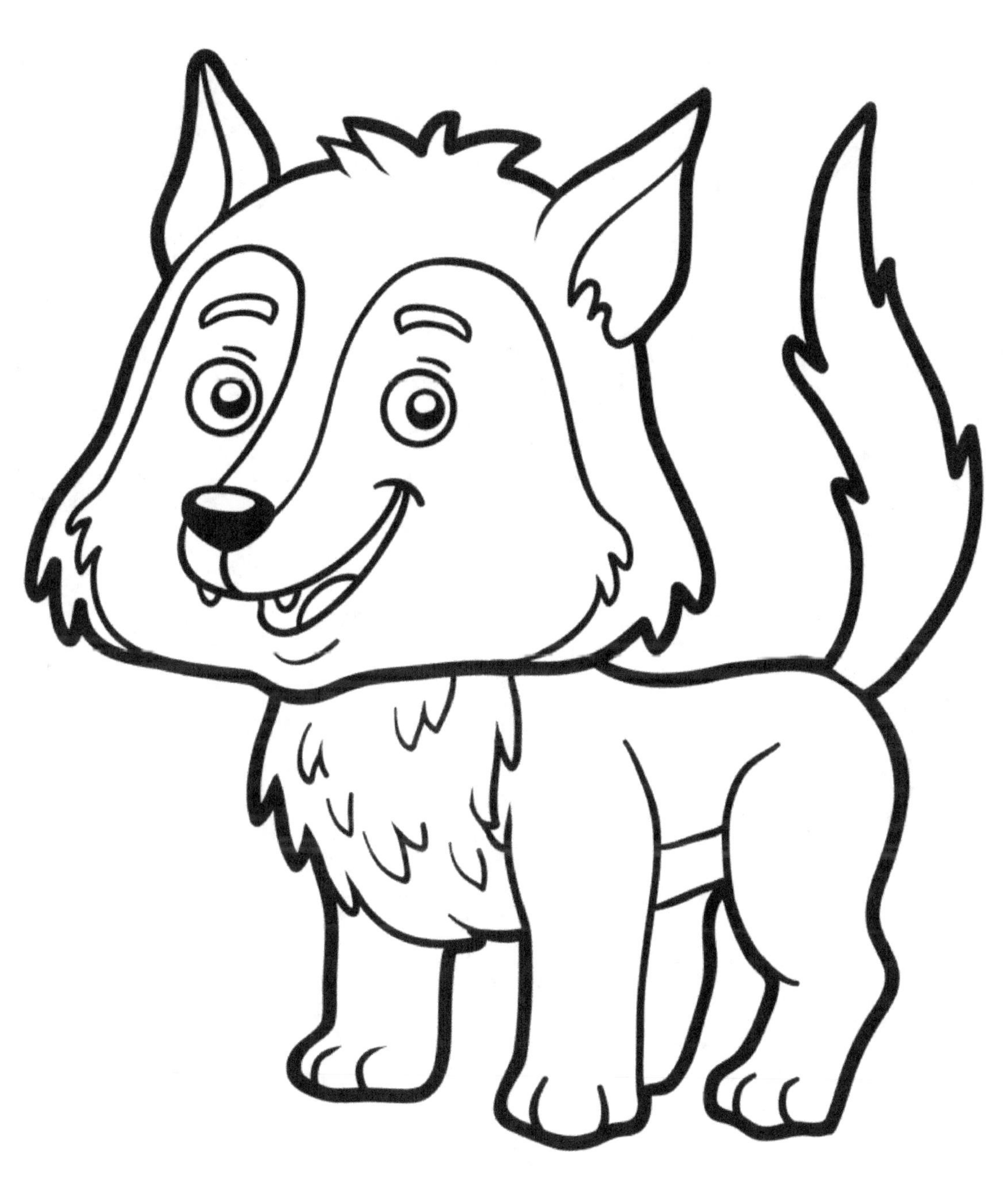

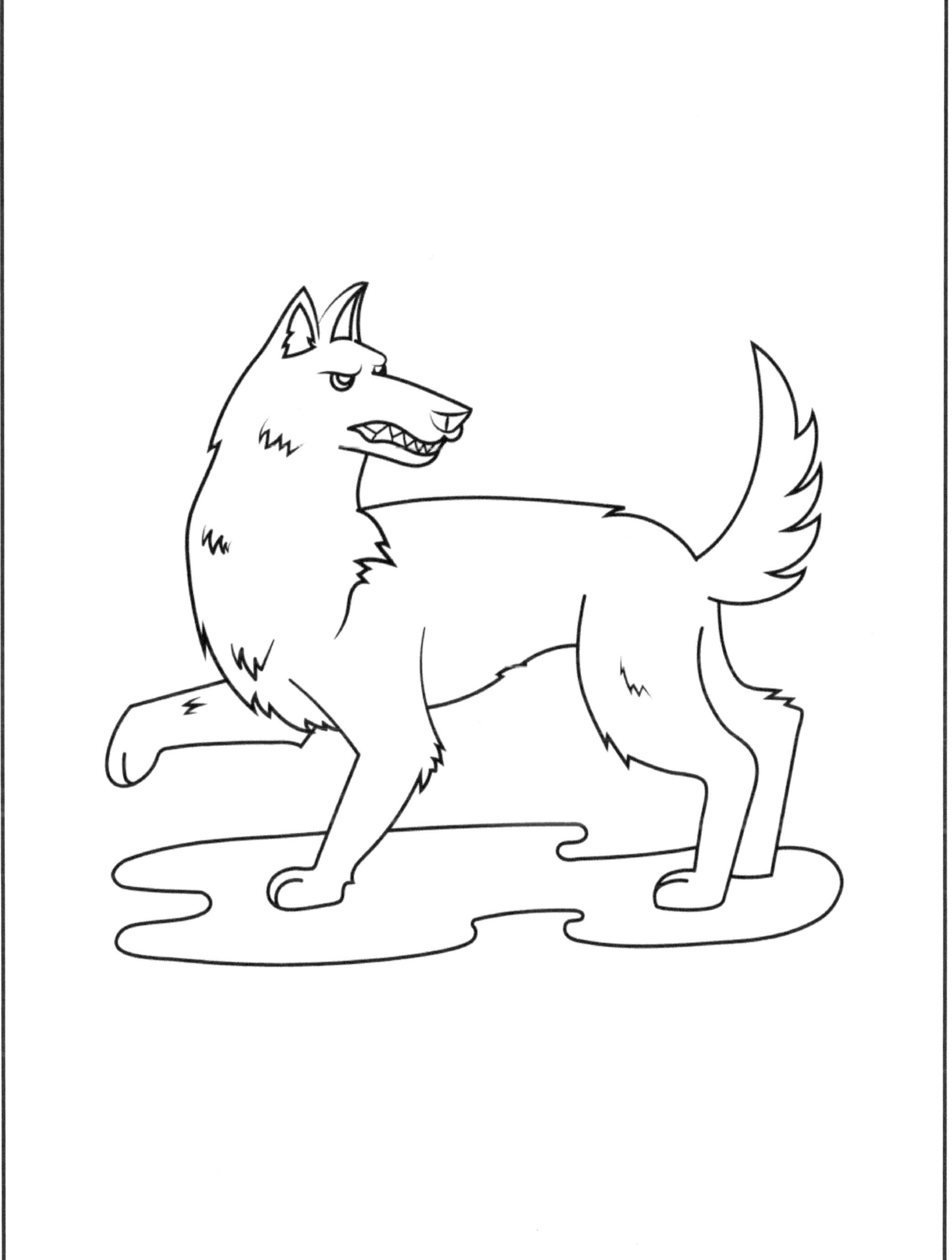

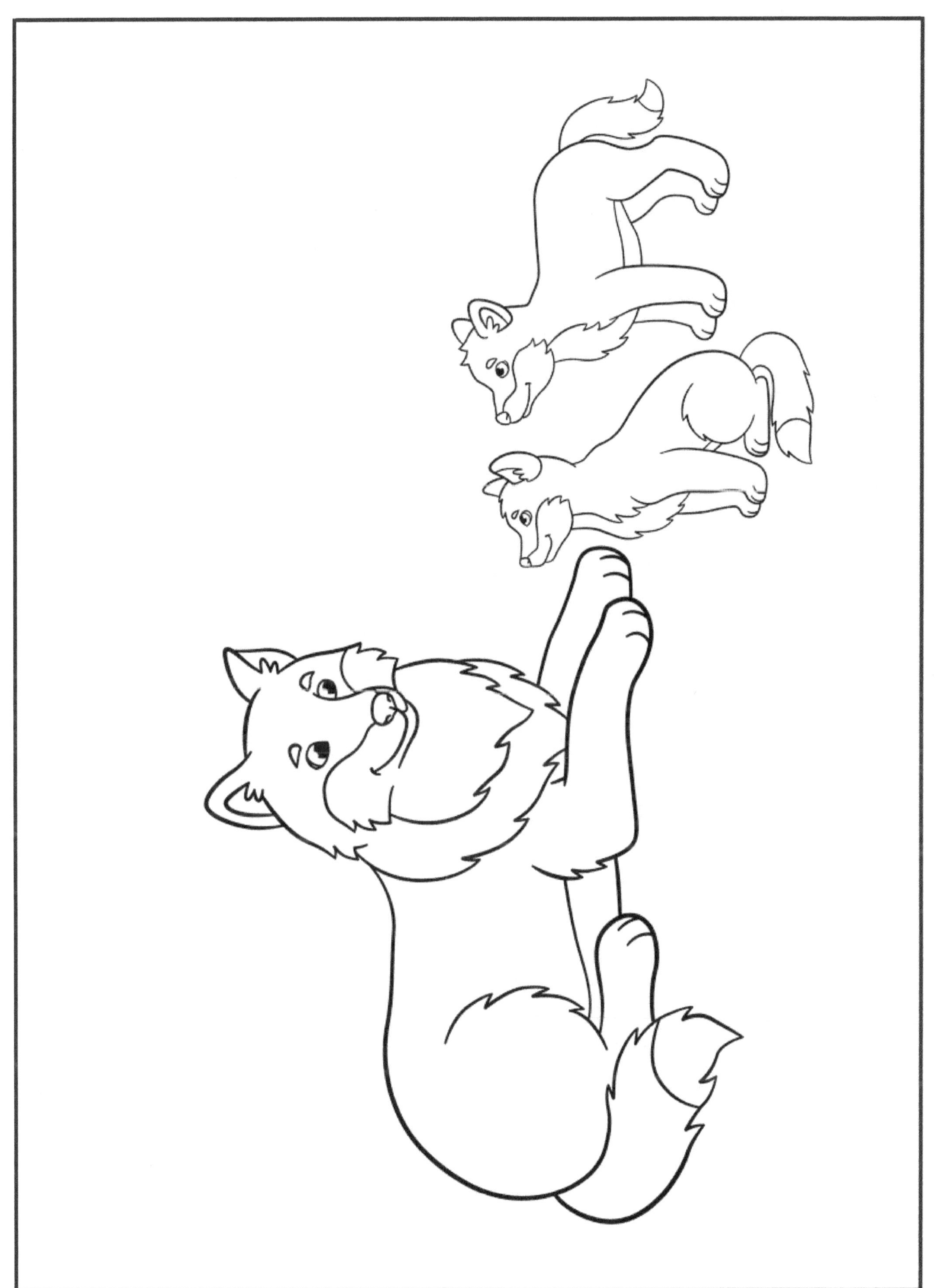

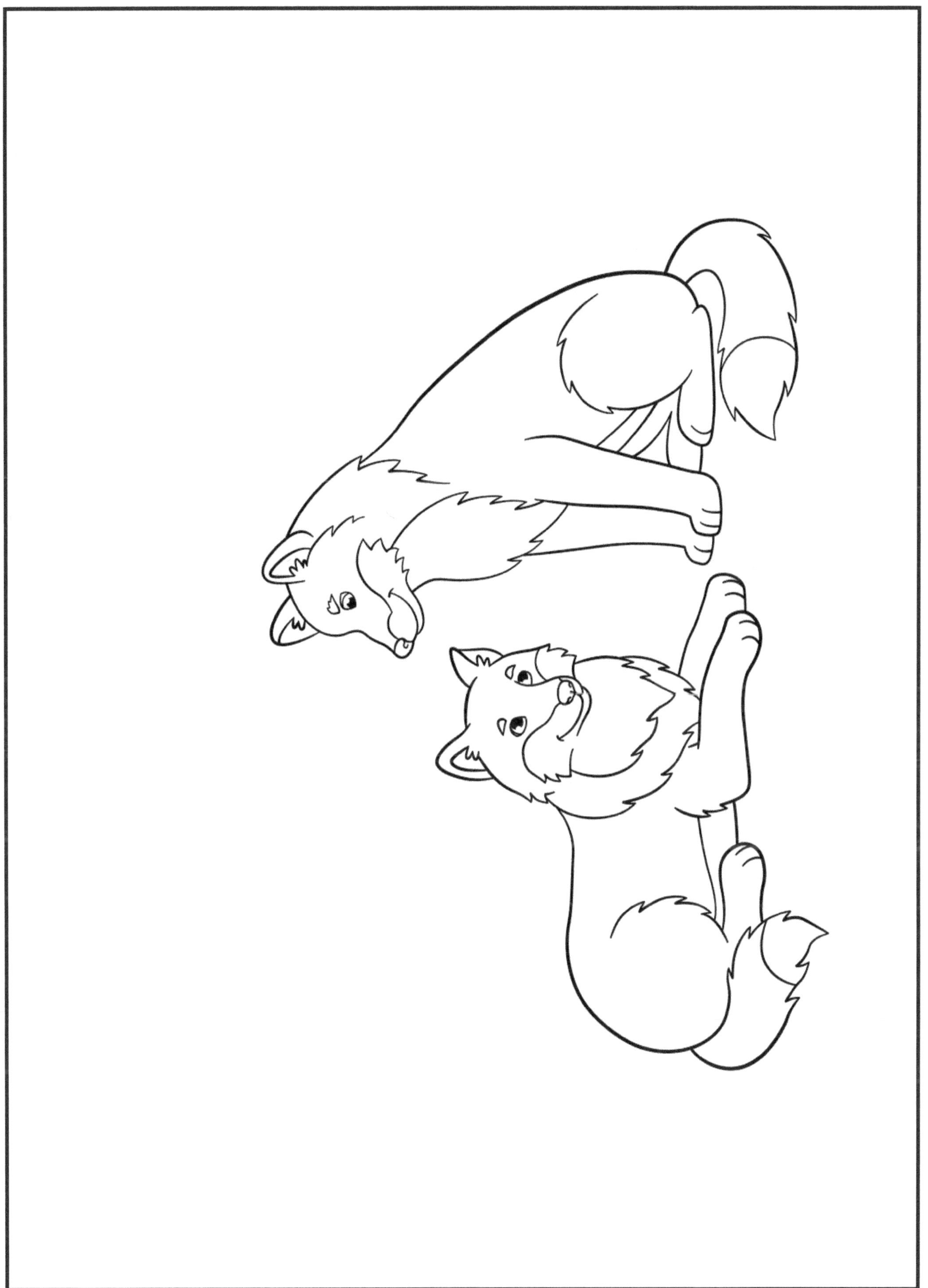

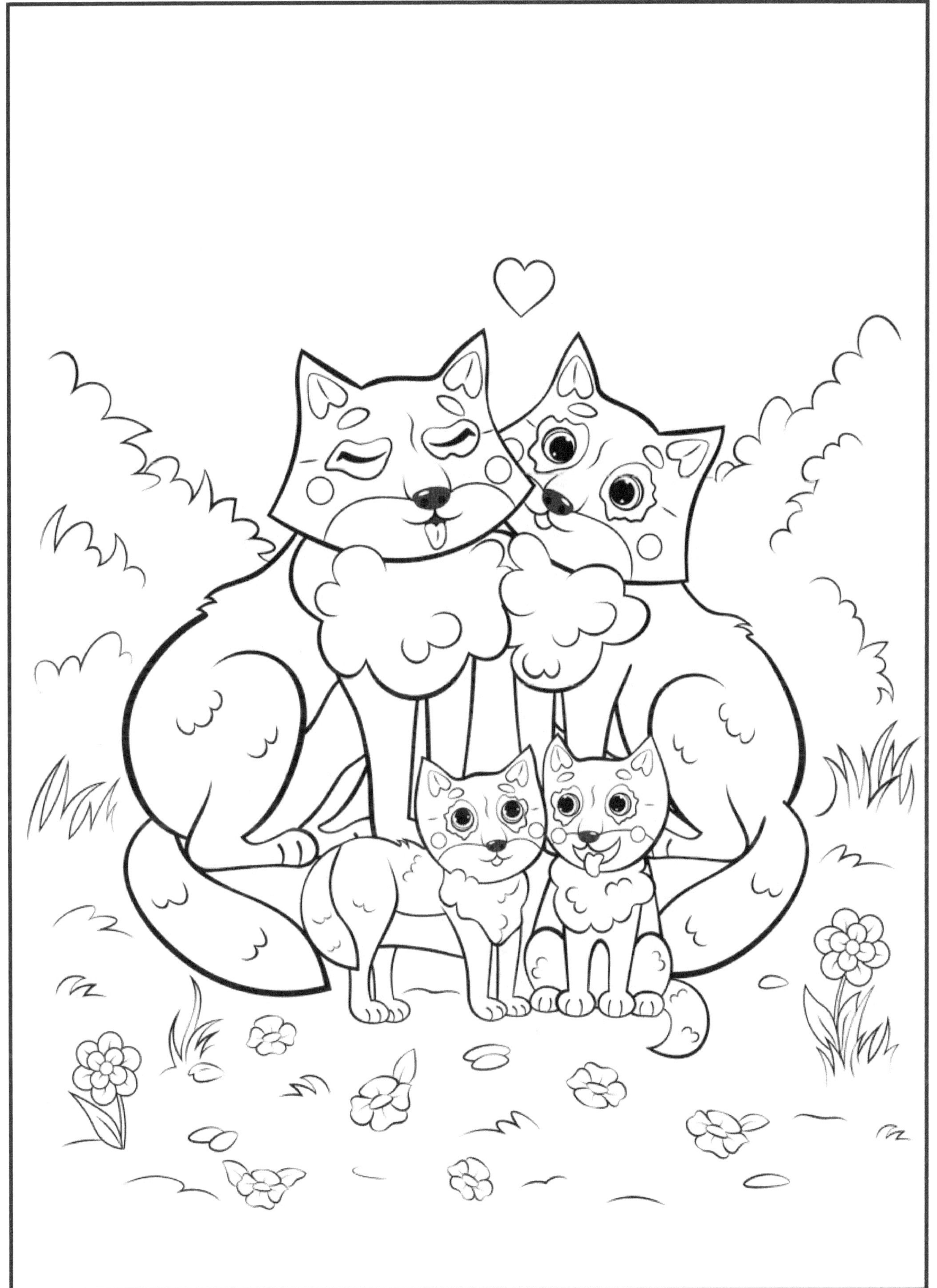

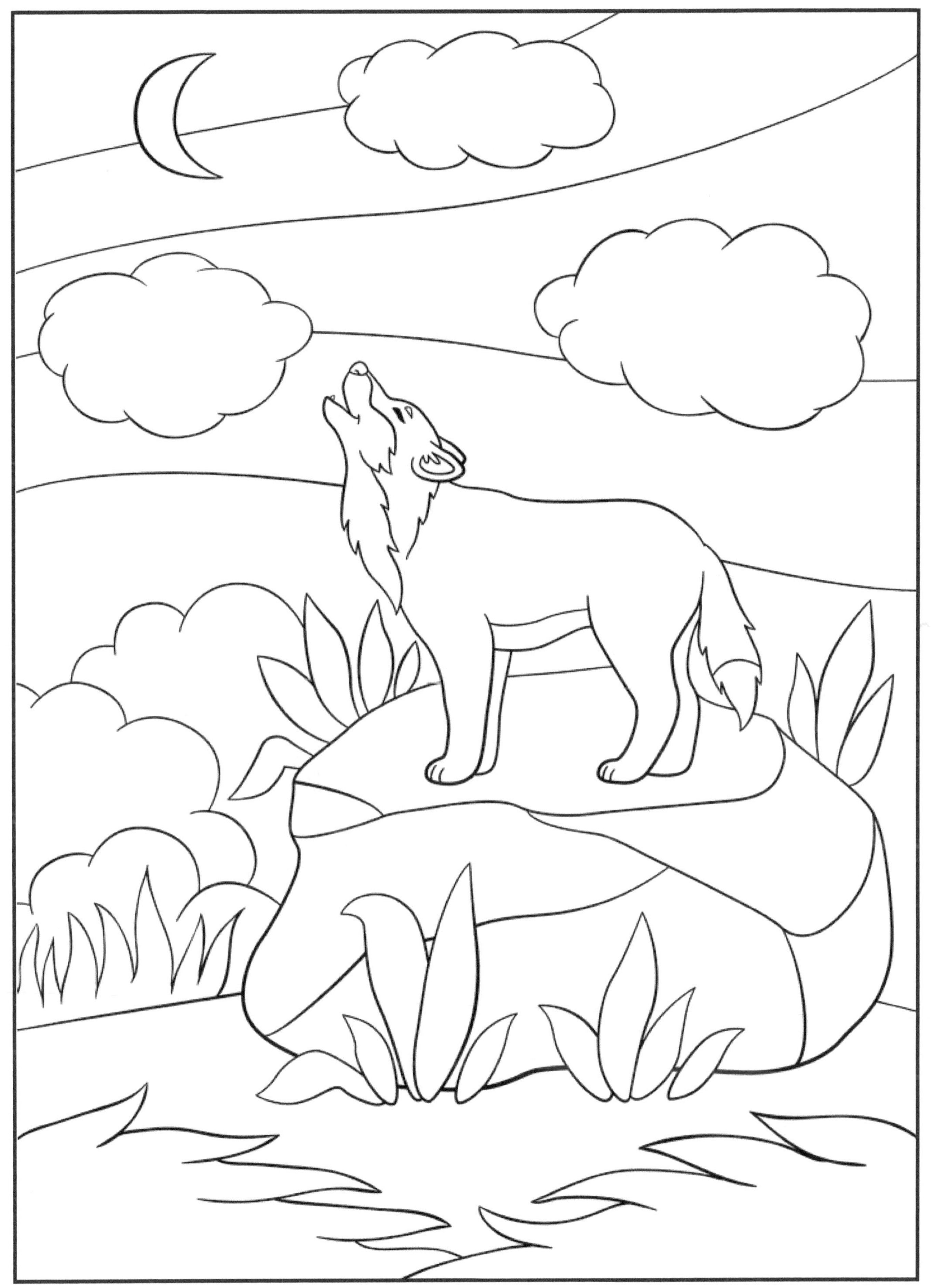

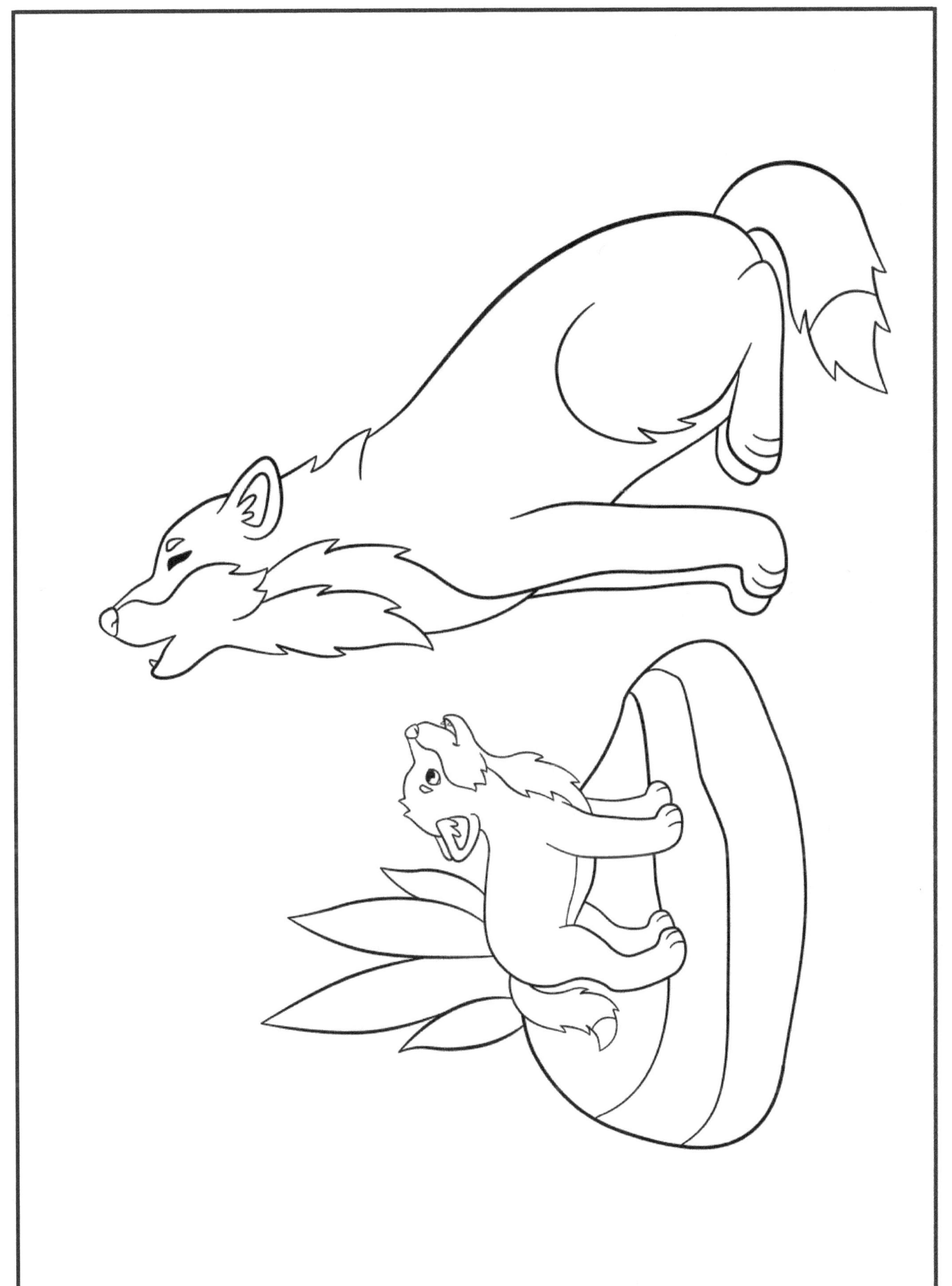

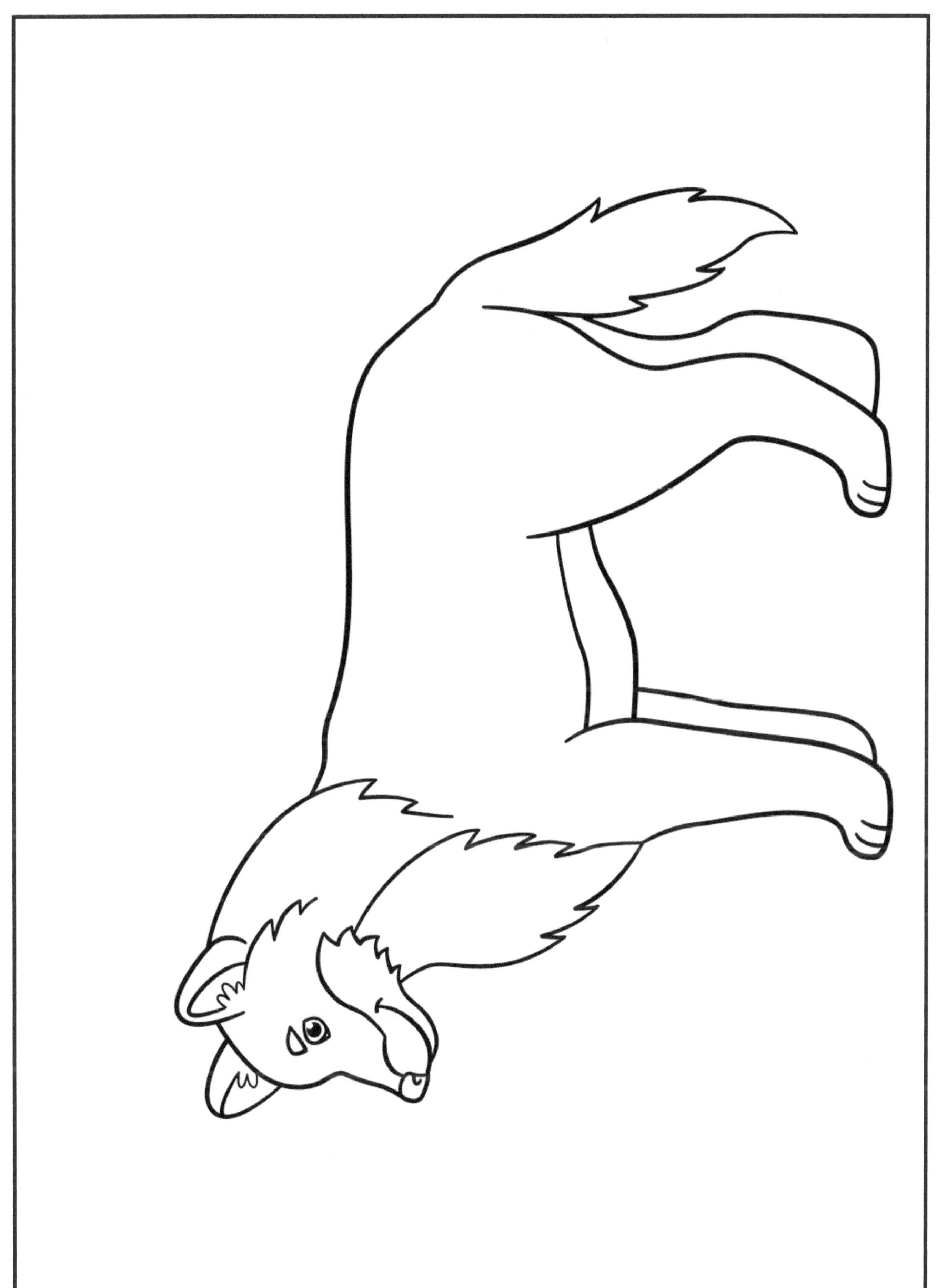

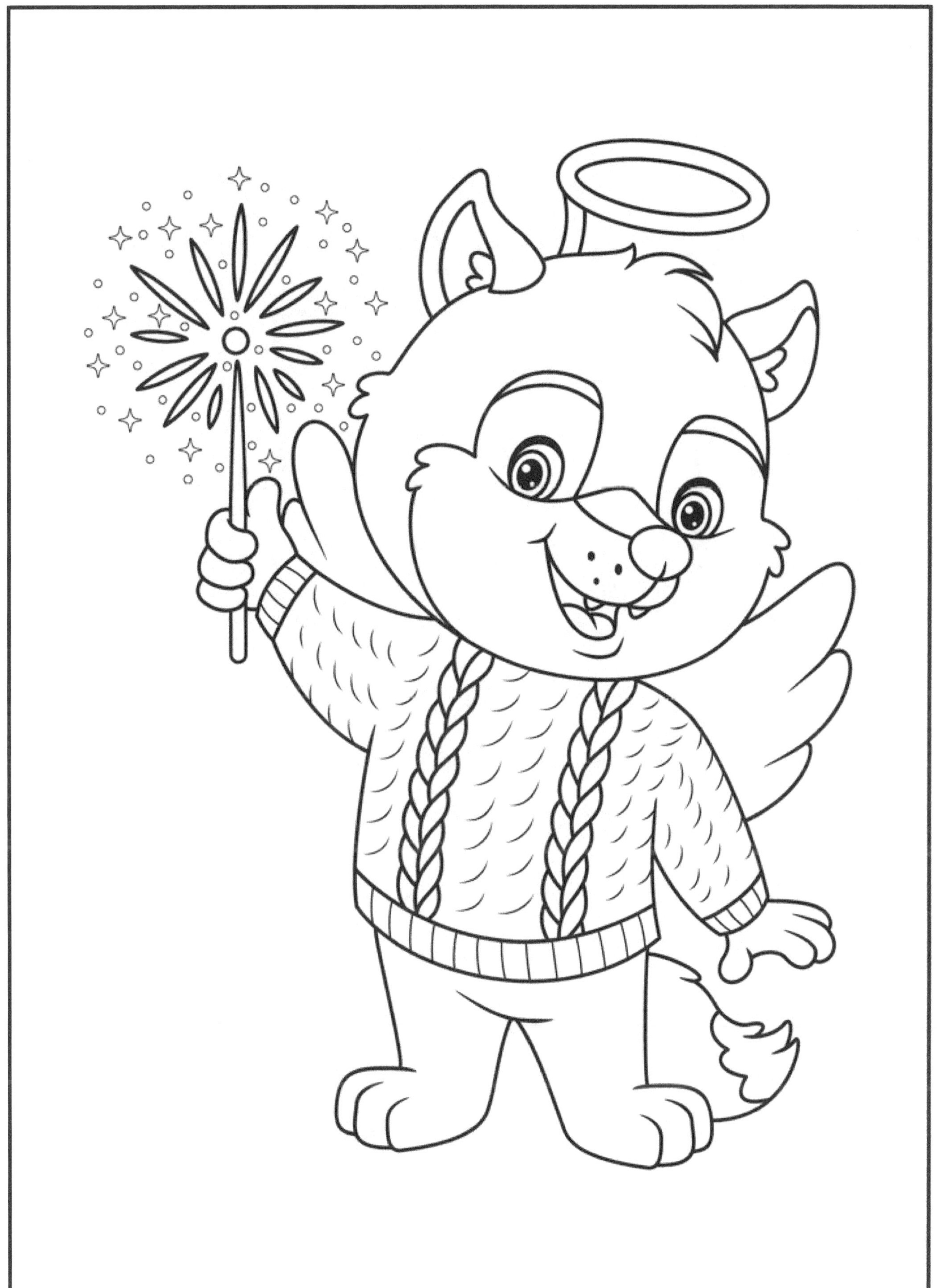

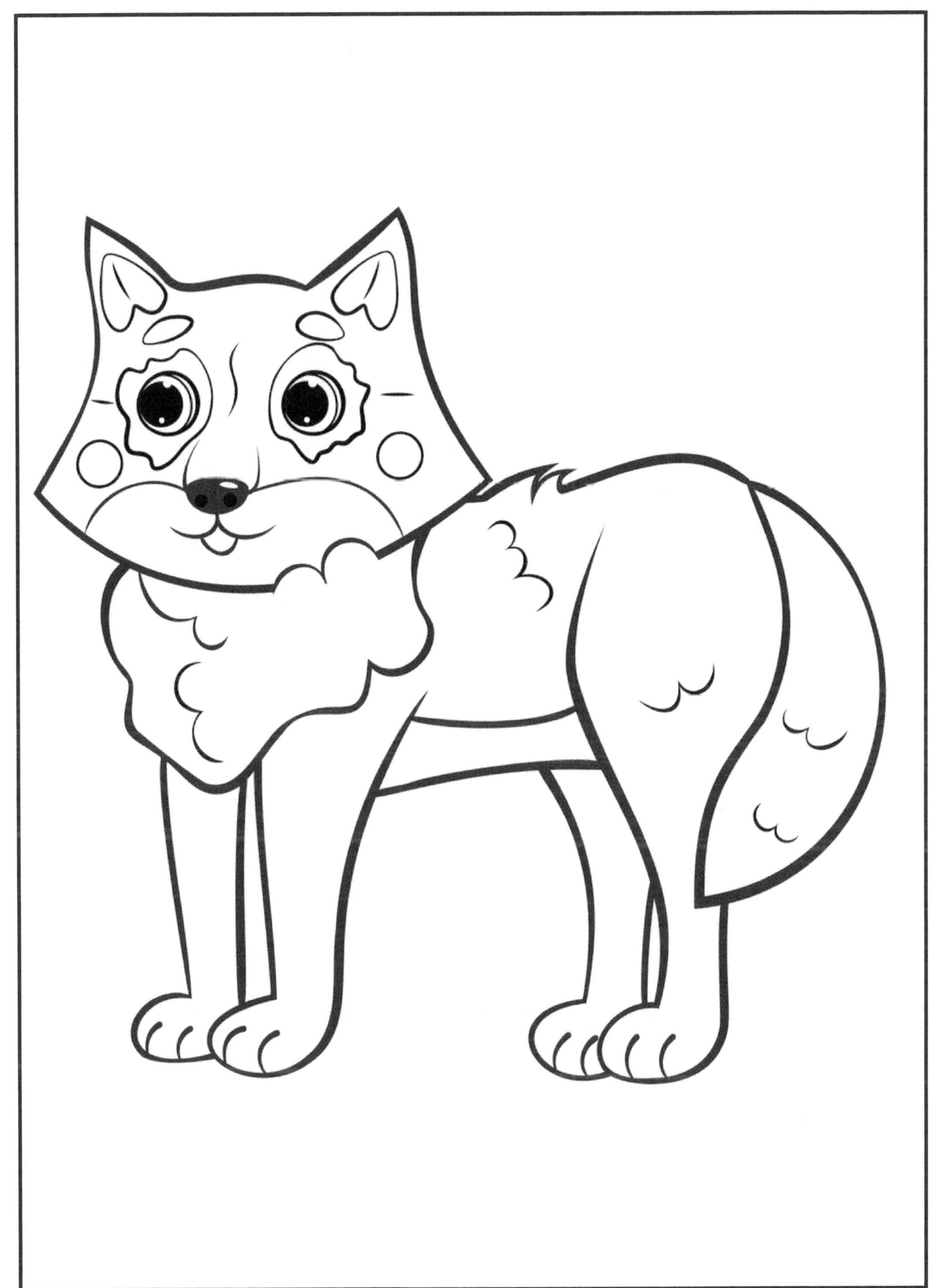

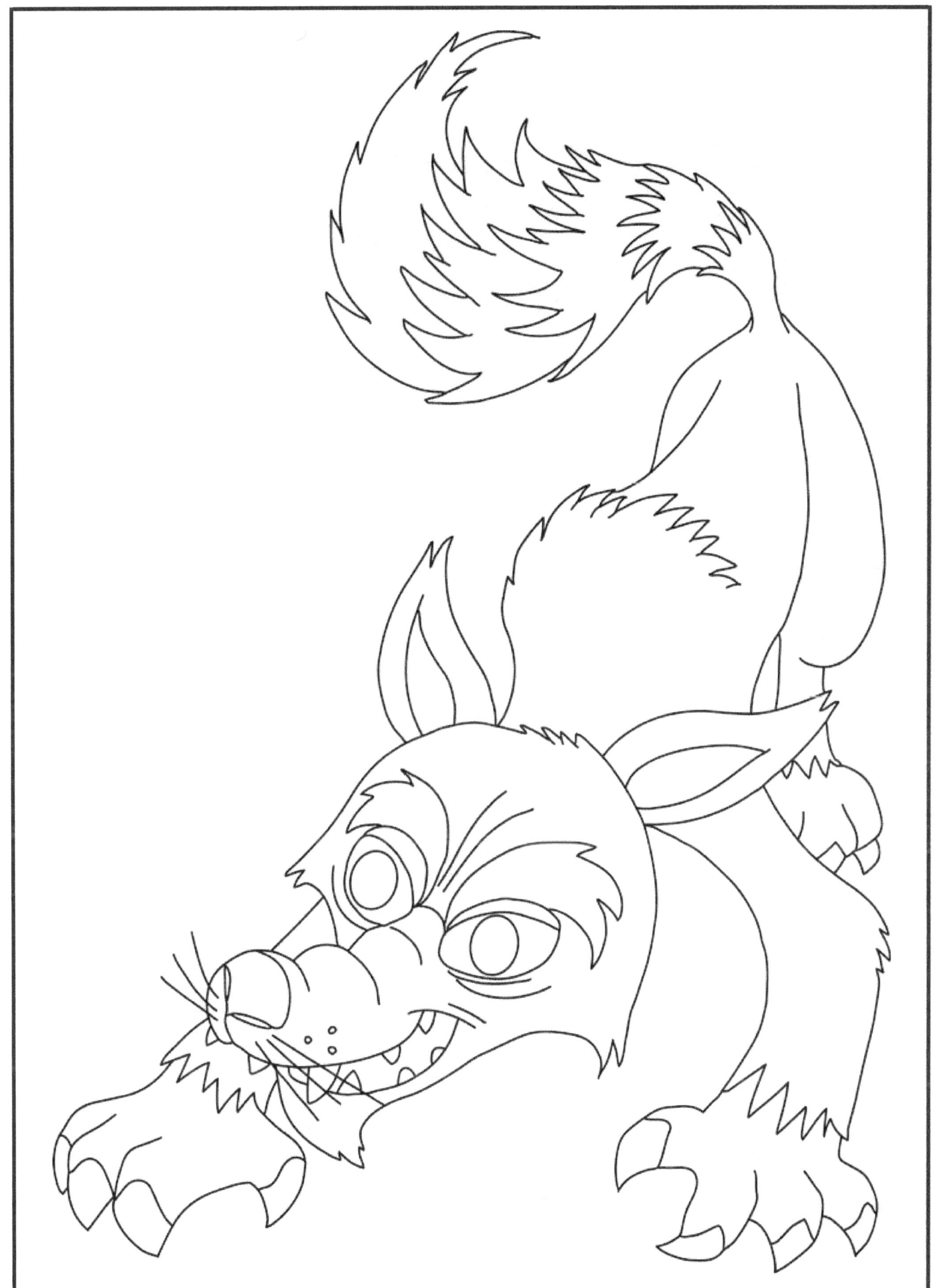

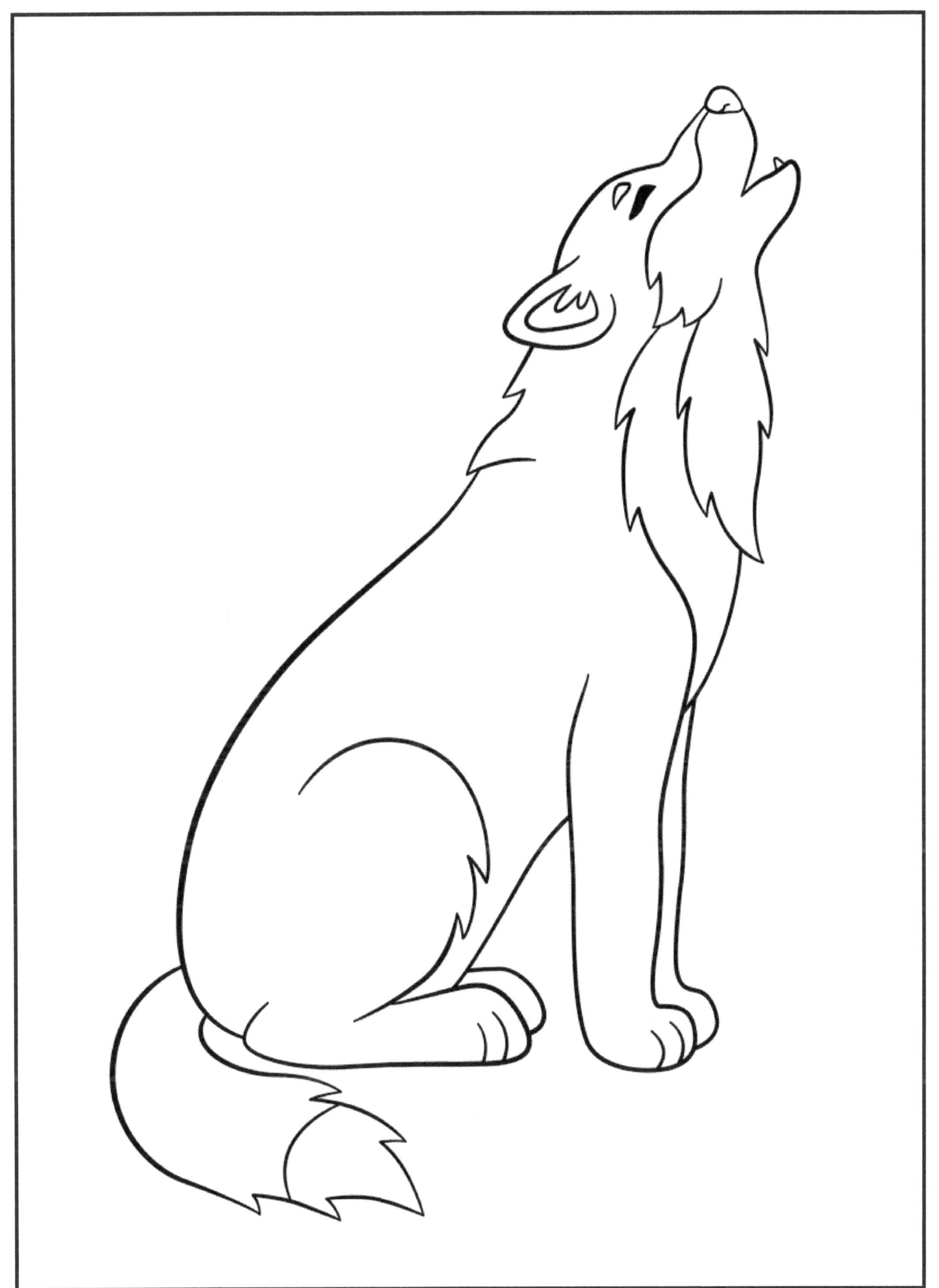

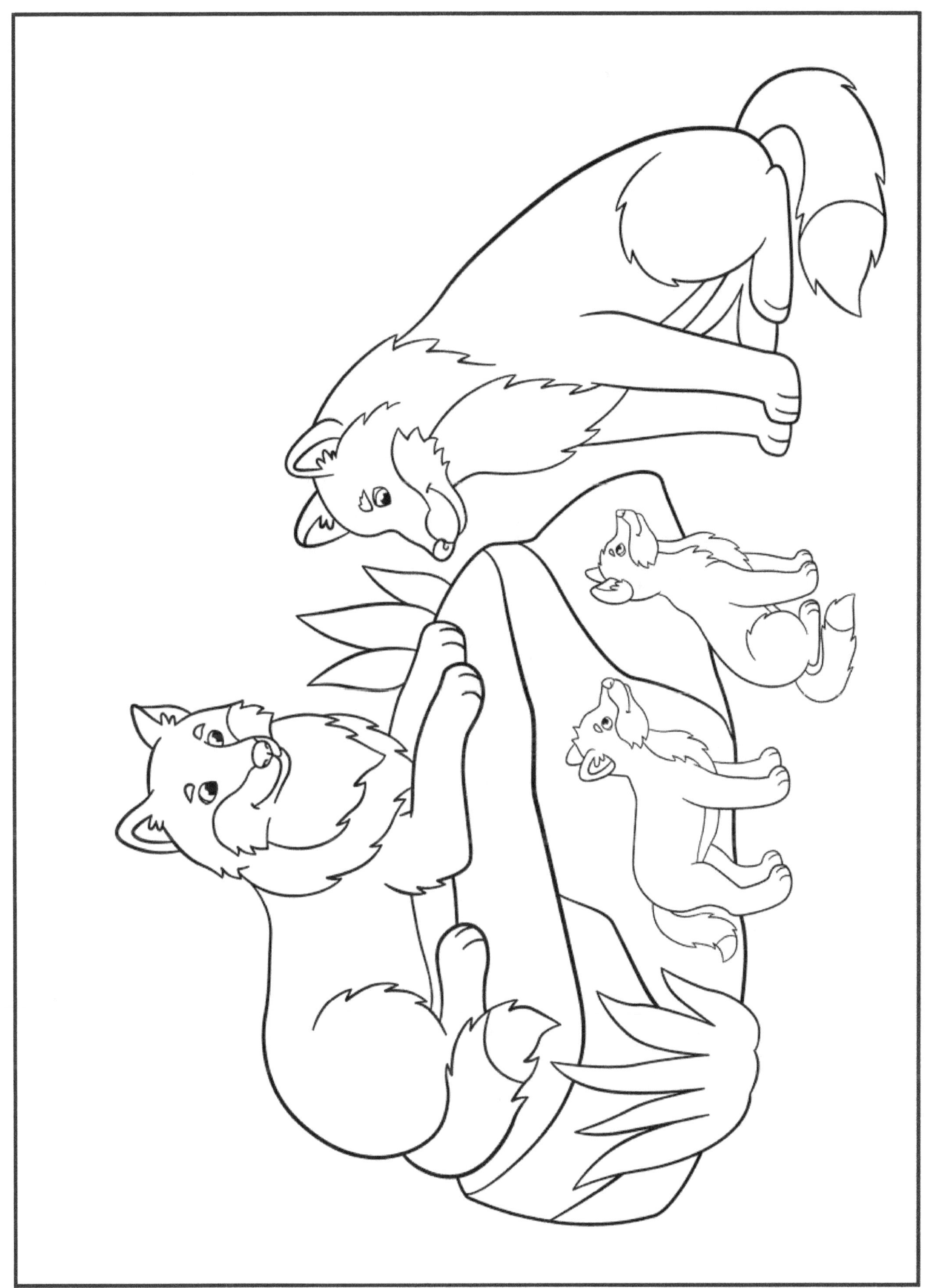

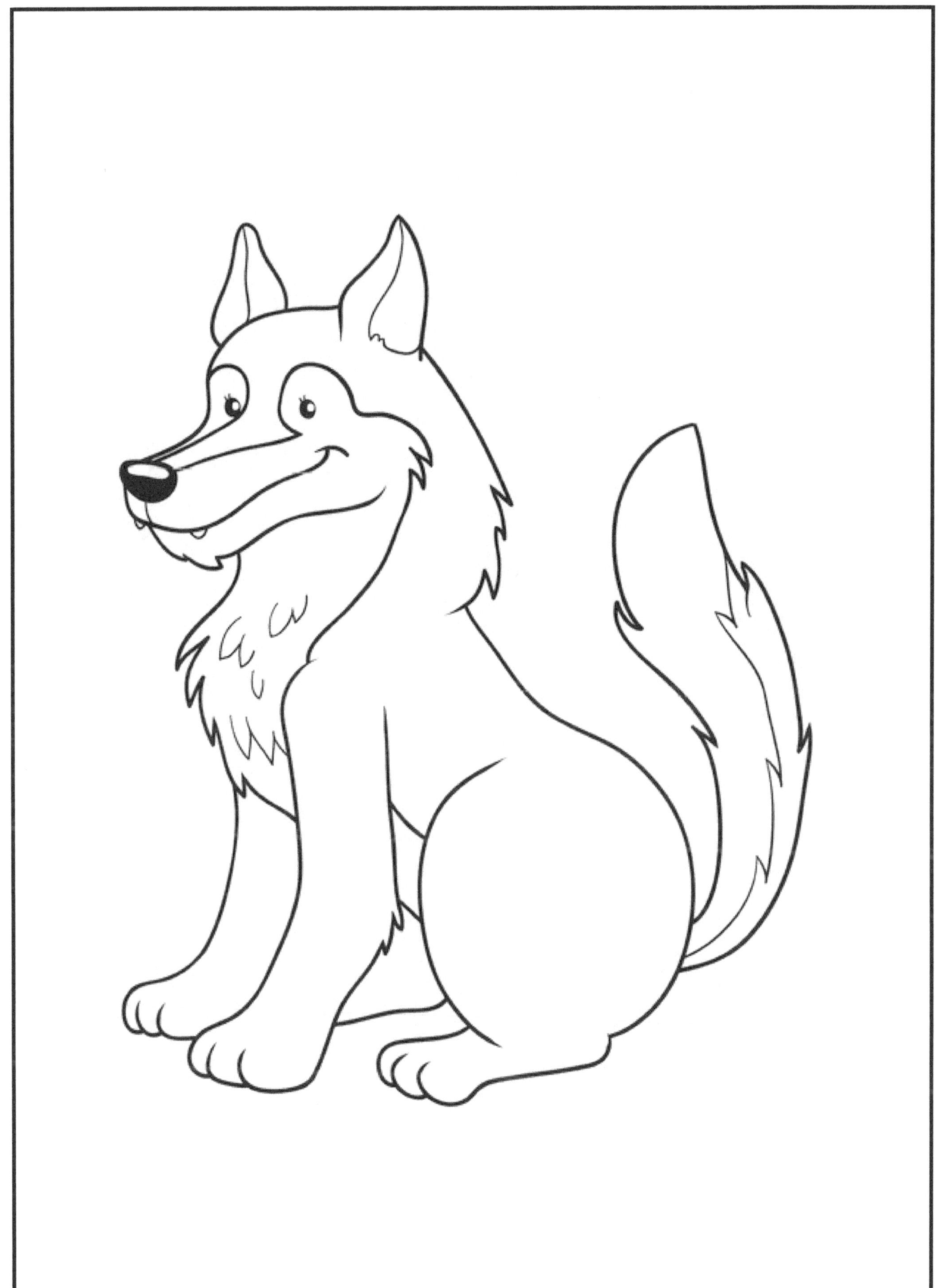

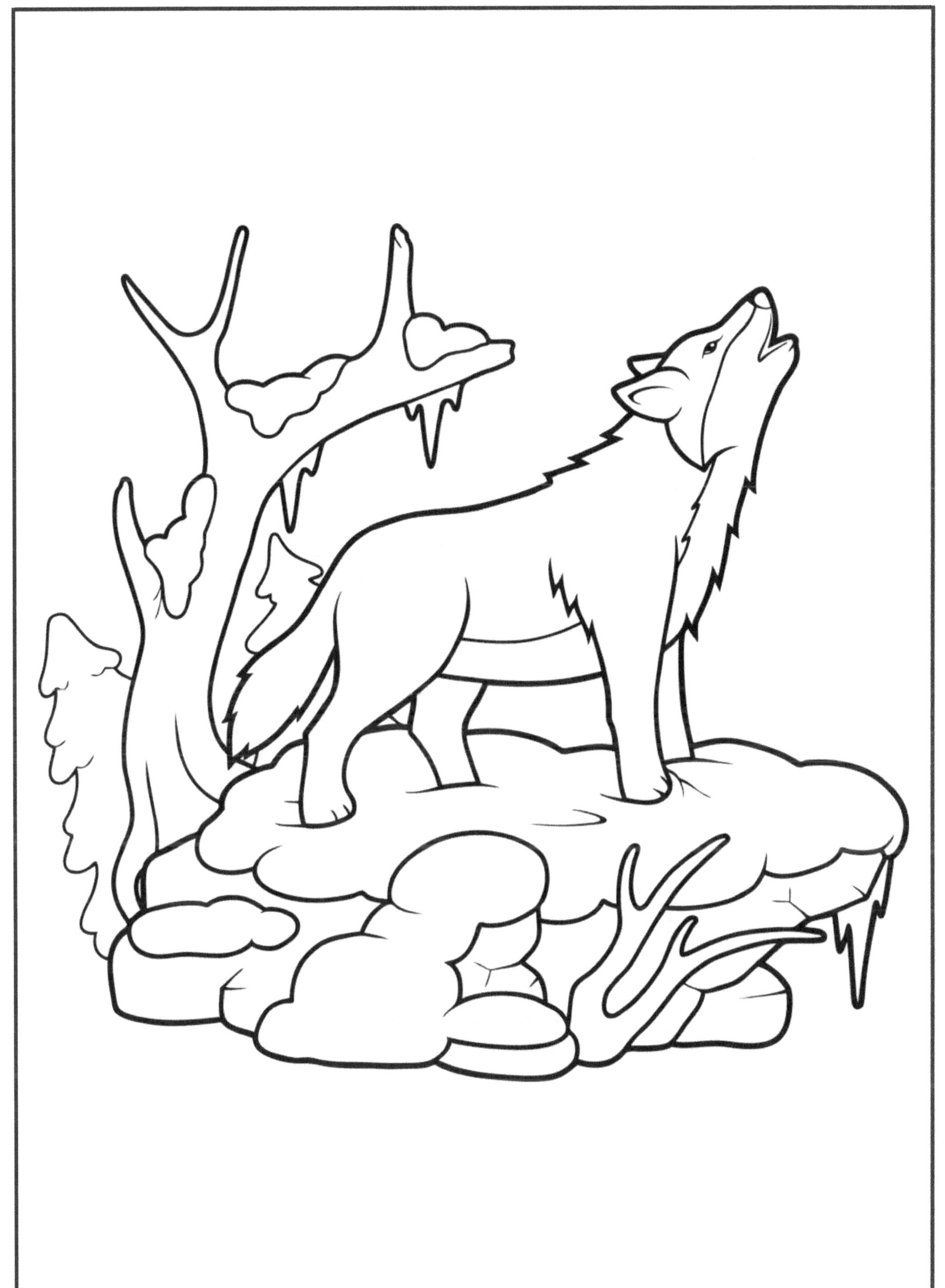

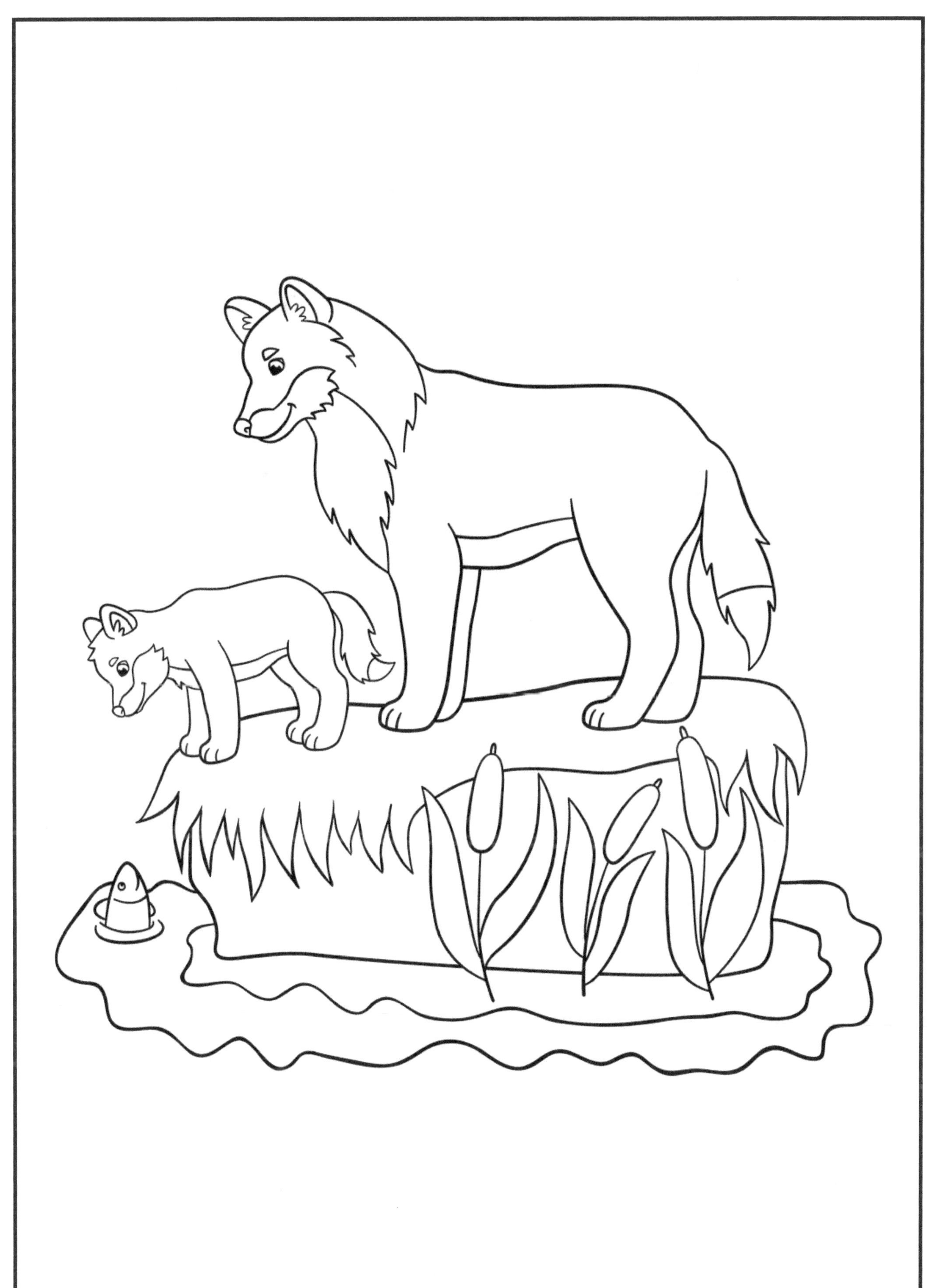

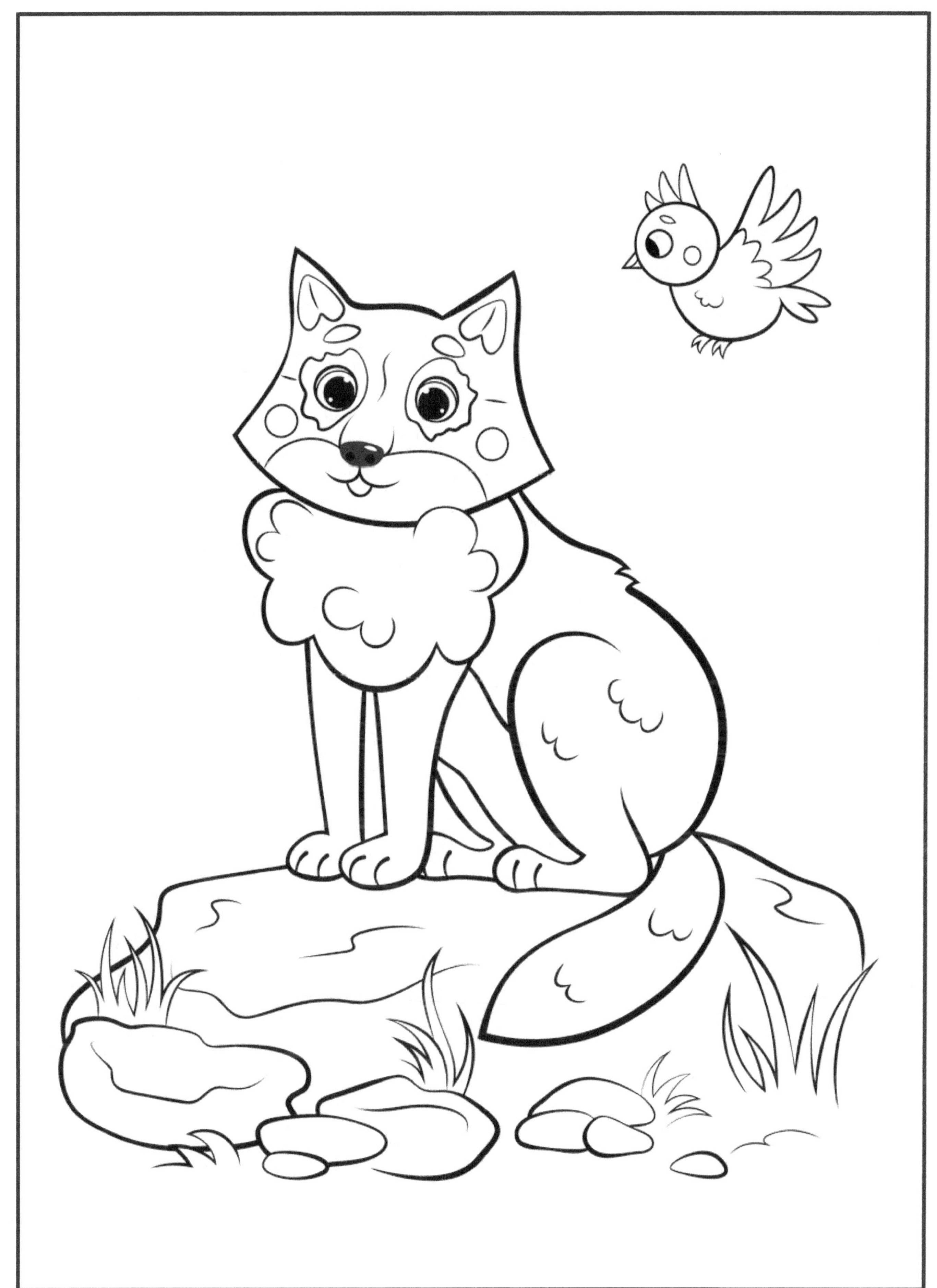

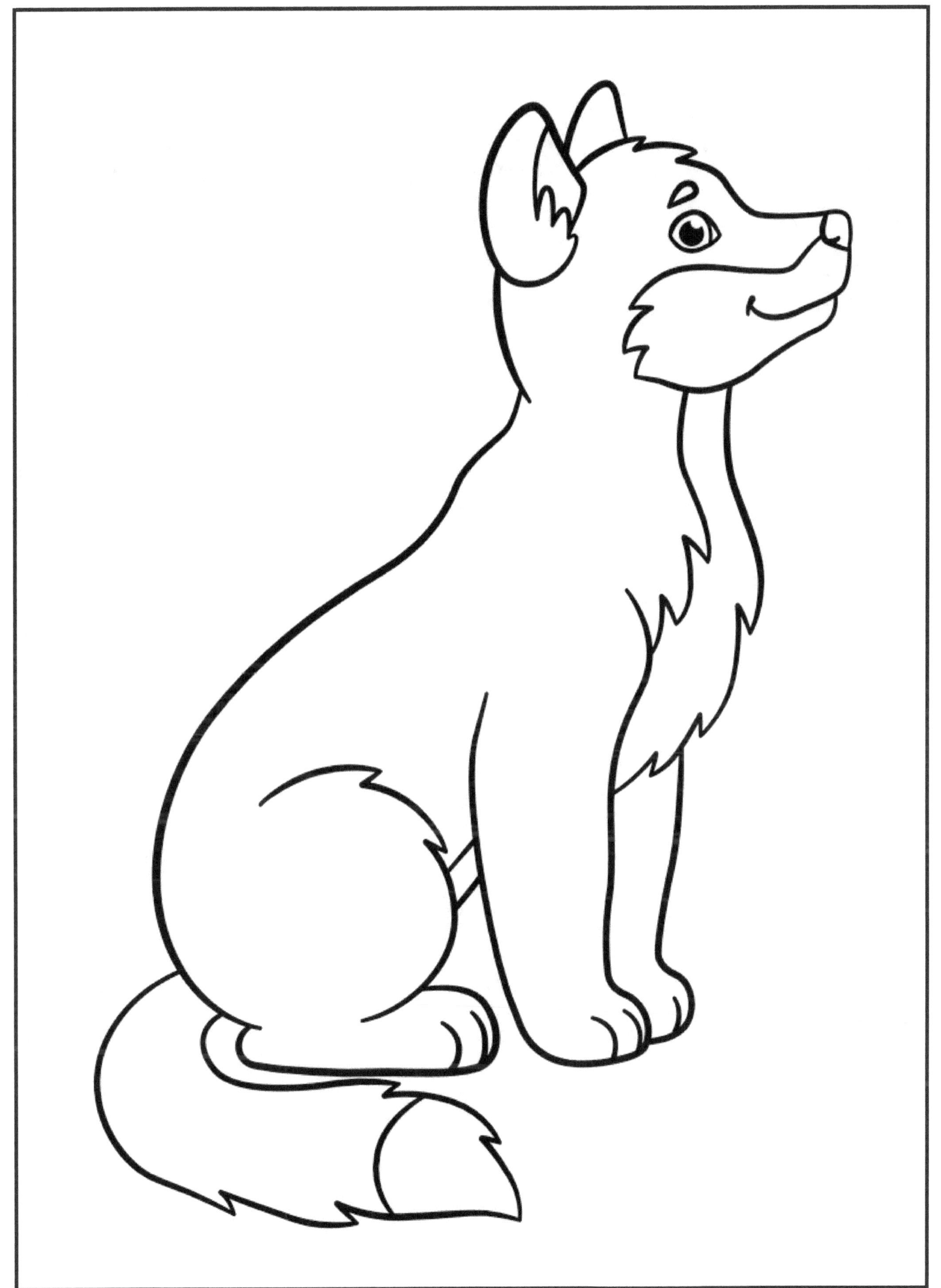

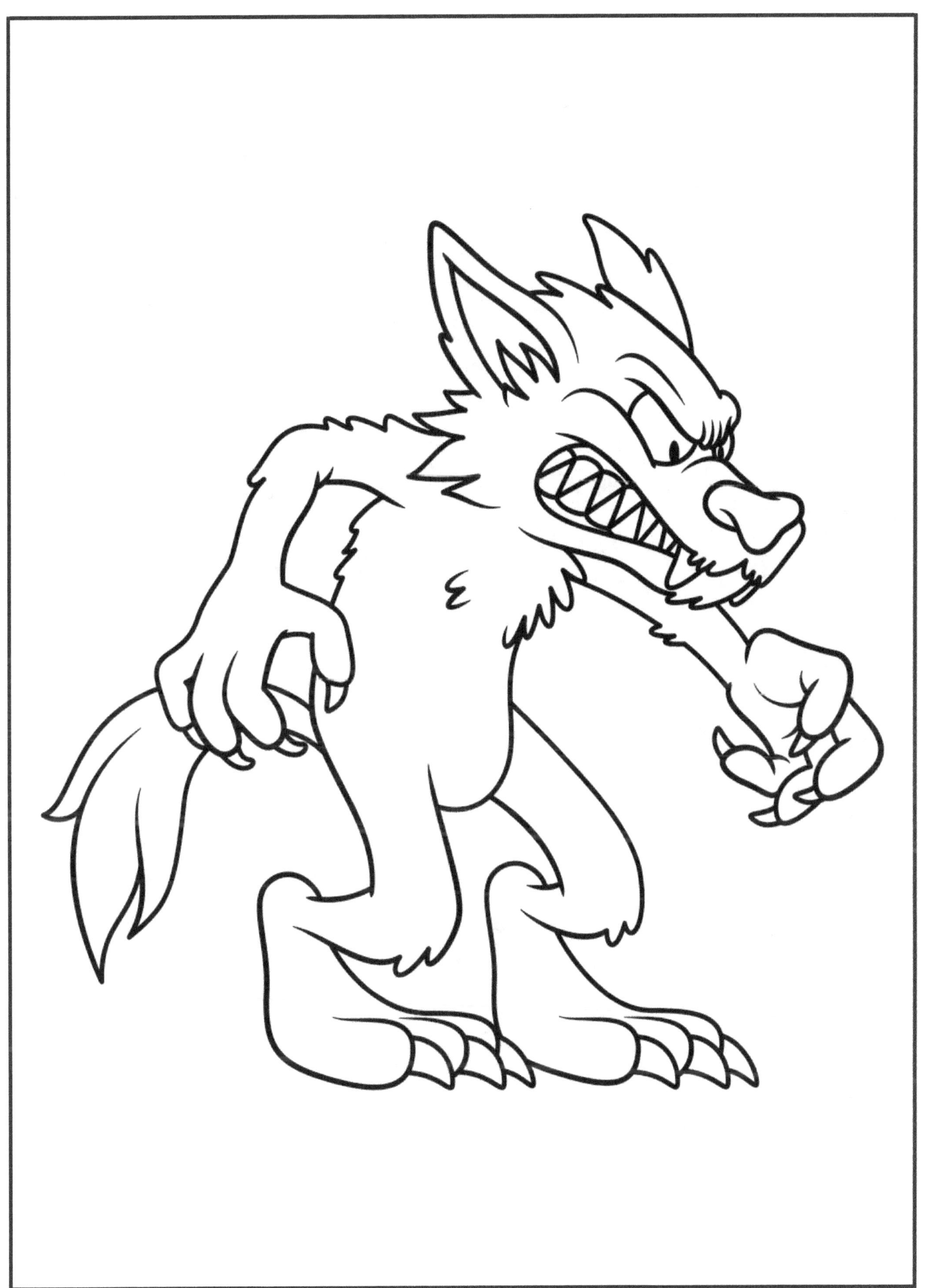

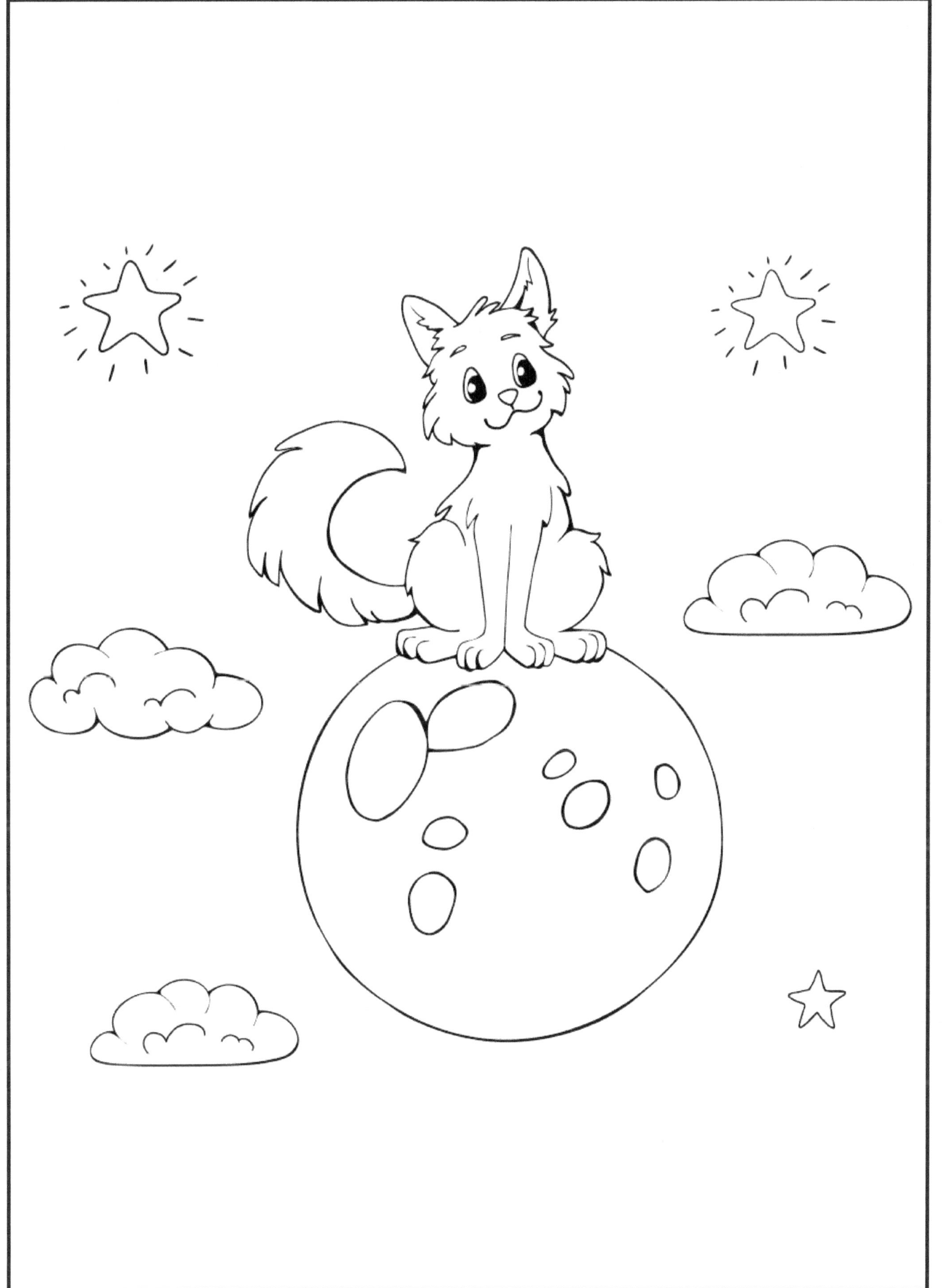

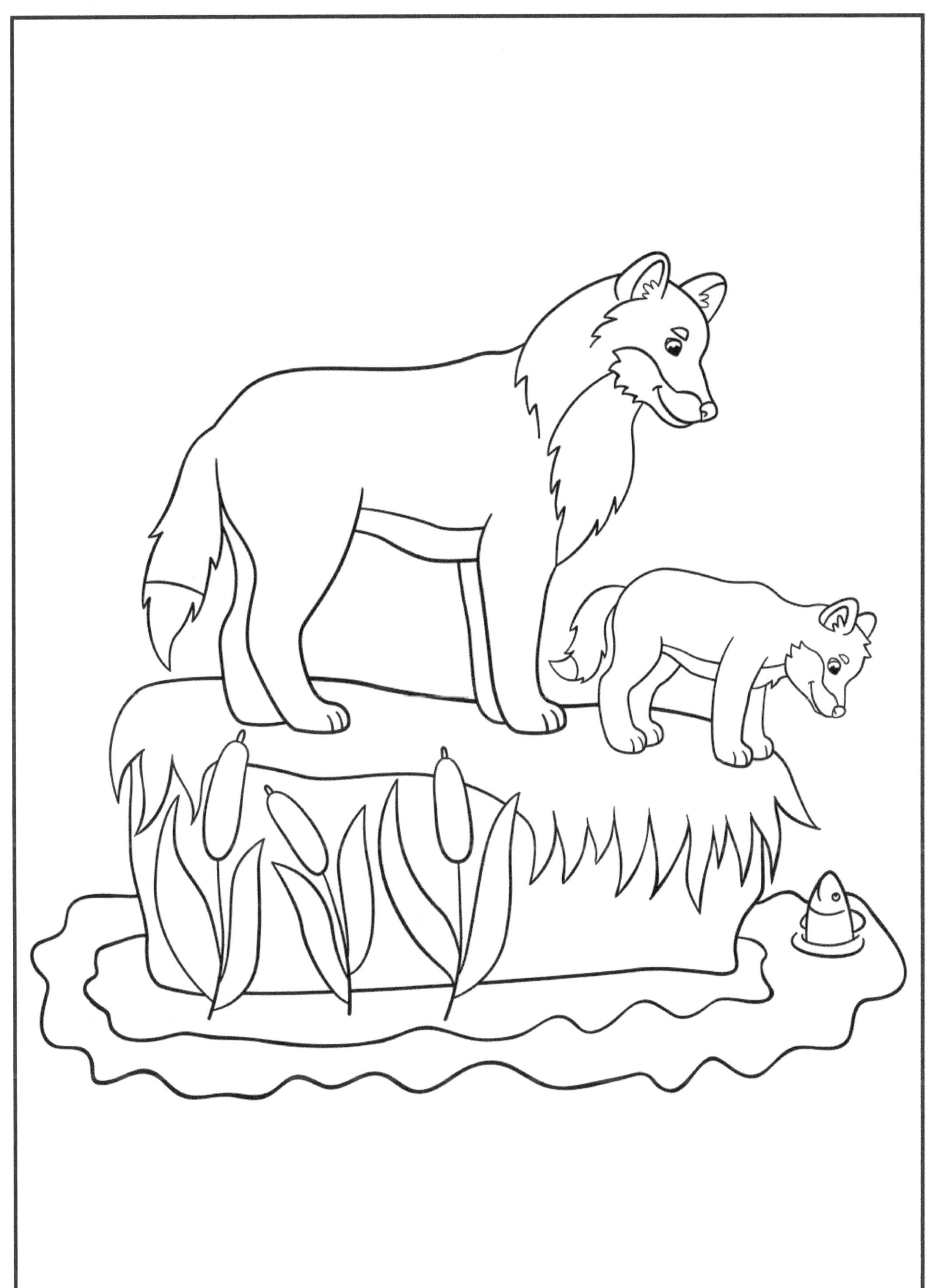

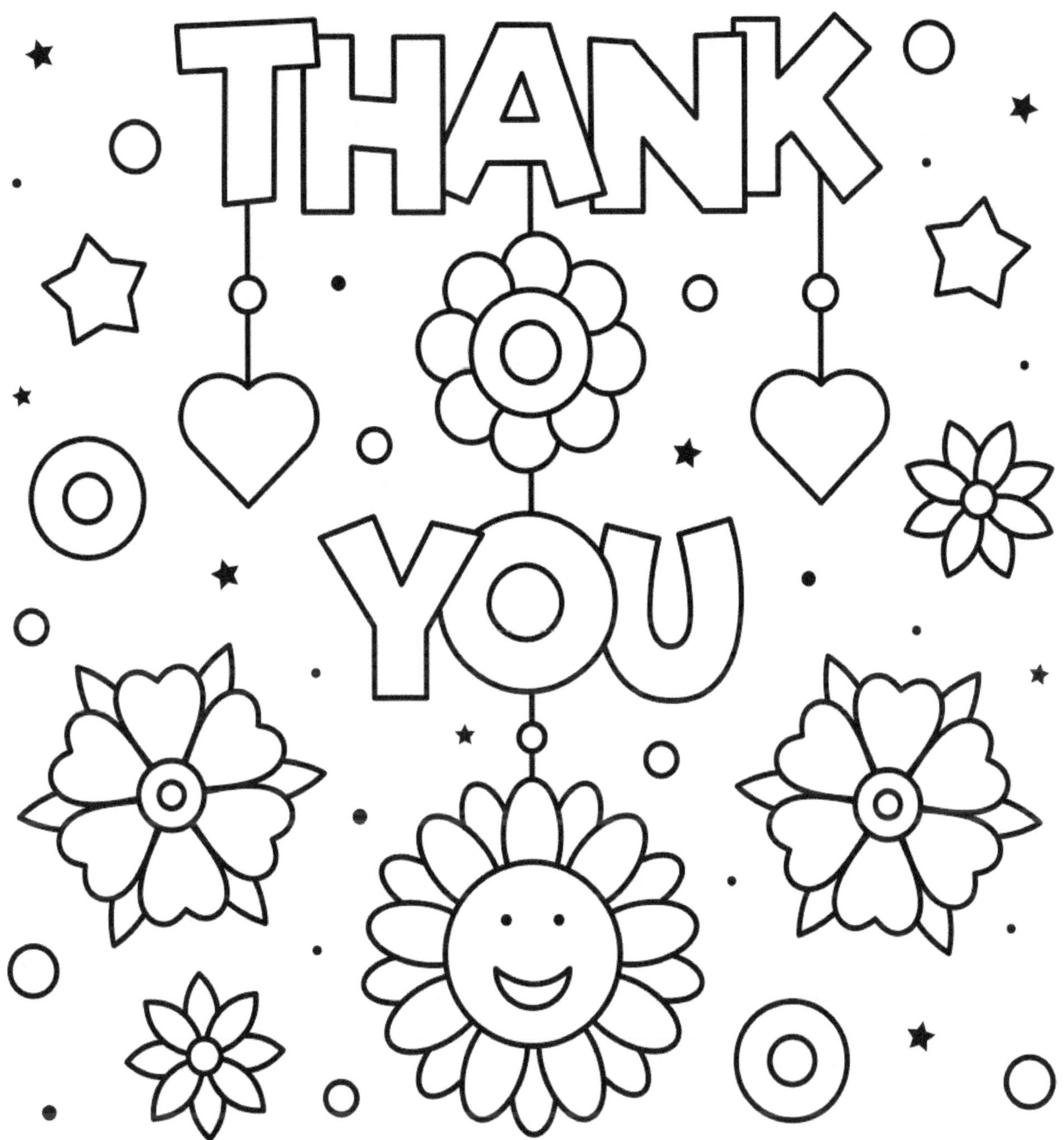

THANK
YOU